Praise for *Naturally Vegetarian*

"Valentina's charming stories and breathtaking images will make you want to hop on a plane to cook alongside her in her Italian countryside kitchen. She somehow combines the incredible ingredients of rural Italy and generations of cooking tradition with modern healthy vegetarian sensibilities in a way that is completely natural, organic, and stunningly beautiful."

—JEANINE DONOFRIO, creator of Love and Lemons
and author of *The Love and Lemons Cookbook*

"This book is pure poetry. Valentina is an artist armed with a wealth of knowledge of Italian cuisine and a passionate approach to food and photography that is truly contagious. *Naturally Vegetarian* opens up a whole world of Italian recipes that are wholesome, inspiring, healthy, and beautiful. This book is a stunning addition to any kitchen."

—MOLLY YEH, creator of My Name is Yeh
and author of *Molly on the Range*

"*Naturally Vegetarian* is far more than a sumptuous collection of vibrant recipes and stunning photographs that conjure the spirit of northeastern Italy: It's a transportive, storytelling work of art that showcases Valentina's passion for food, beauty, and the nourishing connection between humans and the natural world."

—LILY DIAMOND, creator and author of *Kale & Caramel*

Naturally Vegetarian

Naturally Vegetarian

RECIPES & STORIES FROM
MY ITALIAN FAMILY FARM

Valentina Solfrini

AVERY
an imprint of Penguin Random House
New York

AVERY

an imprint of Penguin Random House LLC
375 Hudson Street
New York, New York 10014

Copyright © 2017 Valentina Solfrini
Photographs copyright © Valentina Solfrini

Most Avery books are available at special quantity discounts for bulk purchase for sales promotions, premiums, fund-raising, and educational needs. Special books or book excerpts also can be created to fit specific needs. For details, write SpecialMarkets@penguinrandomhouse.com.

ISBN 9781101983591

Printed in China
1 3 5 7 9 10 8 6 4 2

Book design by Ashley Tucker

CONTENTS

INTRODUCTION

*My family's farmhouse sits on a hill right below the medieval town of Gradara,
a quaint bouquet of houses famous for its top-quality restaurants, its romantic
candlelit alleys, and the massive, elegant Gradara Castle—a storied landmark that
was destroyed and rebuilt after a war between two families in the 1500s.*

I spent my childhood immersed in this fairy tale–like scenery. We have lived on a quiet road on the outskirts of Gradara for generations. Our house, a large ocher building with wooden blinds, is surrounded by fruit and olive yards, almond and walnut trees, and a large field that once hosted a vineyard, which died along with my great-grandfather. From our farmhouse, you can see the Adriatic Sea stretch far at each end of the scenery, from the southern hilly coast of Le Marche, carpeted in woods and green fields, to the flat Emilia-Romagna region in Northeastern Italy.

Gradara is right on the border between these two distinct regions—each with its own dialect, history, and cuisine. A few miles to the west, Emilia-Romagna is famous for its iconic dishes and ingredients. Much of what people think of as "Italian food" comes from here: Parmigiano-Reggiano, Bolognese sauce, prosciutto di Parma. Italians agree, as much as we can agree on anything related to food, that Emilia-Romagna's cuisine is one of the greatest in all of Italy. South of our farm is the Marche region, an unspoiled, rural region between the Apennine Mountains and the Adriatic coast. Le Marche is filled with medieval villages and the land is hilly, gradually sloping toward the sea. Its cuisine is lesser-known than Emilia-Romagna's but just as delicious, bristling with the flavors left behind by thousands of years of invasions.

Meat features strongly in the cuisine of both areas. A typical meal starts with salami and a selection of cured meats, followed by pasta served with sausage or filled with a mixture of ground beef, pork, and charcuterie. Sauces are made with chicken giblets or browned chicken liver. Pork and chicken are prevalent in the mountains, and seafood dominates on the coast.

Yet it's from the intersection of these regions that I cook and write about plant-based food. In a back room of our farmhouse, in an unused space filled with old furniture and beautiful light, I photograph and write my blog, *Hortus Cuisine*.

How did I become a standard-bearer for vegetarian Italian cuisine? Quite by accident. I am not a trained chef, and still today I do enjoy the occasional local seafood and traditional cheeses, which makes me more of a supporter of a mostly plant-based way of eating rather than a full vegetarian.

As the daughter of a farming family, I grew up eating the seasonal, fresh food prepared by my mother and grandmother, who were both professional cooks. My life was filled with homemade food and cooking, and it was not often that we set foot in a restaurant. My grandmother and my mother alike didn't really trust other people to prepare their food.

My grandma worked as a pasta maker at Bologna's fairs, and she could roll a sheet of dough out thin like no one else. She'd say that if you make pasta in Bologna, it has to be thin enough that you can see St. Peter's Cathedral through it. Likewise, my mom has worked as a cook in restaurants and hotels all her life. She started out at eleven in a pastry shop where she could not even reach the counter and had to stand on a little stool. With two women like that in the house, it was no wonder I would learn a thing or two about cooking! It was such a basic and everyday part of life.

But it was all something I took for granted. My passion wasn't food but art. For years, I studied design and illustration. My teachers said I had promise and encouraged me. When I graduated, I wanted to experience the vibe of a big city, to discover new things for my art and my future. So I packed my bags, said good-bye to my family, and moved to New York. What city could possibly be better?

I loved the chaos, the people, and even the smells. And I was amused by the American idea of Italian cooking: Garlic powder—a flavor I had never really experienced, was liberally used in every tomato sauce I came across. I found cheeses everywhere in supermarkets labeled as Italian that did not taste one bit Italian, and everyone thought Alfredo sauce was actually a real thing, when in Italy it is not. I remember how I told an American food-lover I met that I thought garlic powder was a distinctly American flavor. He said, "That's funny. People here think garlic powder is a distinctly Italian flavor!" I face-palmed myself. It was a seemingly endless, yet incredibly fun, learning process and window into the way other cultures try to translate a cuisine.

One of the things that struck me the most about the city was that cooking was largely seen as a task rather than a pleasure. It surprised me how little the average New Yorker cooked at home. But in this new place with all new influences, I finally had a chance to test my own cooking. I experimented in my tiny kitchen in a 270-square-foot apartment in Yorkville for a few hours most evenings after a long day of work. I visited every hidden and known food shop I could possibly find in both Brooklyn and the city, and walked up and down the seemingly endless cookbook aisles in bookstores. I found some authentic preparations of Italian dishes— gnocchi and ravioli, doused in truffle and cheese sauce or fried in butter and sage—and I learned that Italian wines, pecorino cheeses, and sott'oli had their own place in the New York gastronomy scene. I realized that many American cooks did not know that sautéing pasta straight in the pan with a tablespoon or two of the pasta cooking water would produce an infinitely better pasta bowl, and that there was a world of ingredients I was not familiar with that make sense in Italian cooking. These new experiences and tastes, combined with the wisdom I'd learned, gave a whole new meaning to the very act of cooking.

Thinking about how vegetables were valued in my family, I naturally started to veer toward the flavors I remembered from my vegetable garden back in Italy. I cooked with vegetables more and more, and with meat less and less.

What one can do with such variety of flavors, textures, and colors!

As I sought out new recipes and food sources, I stumbled across a vibrant community of vegetarians. To my surprise, they weren't eating too much tofu and meat substitutes, but instead were sharing delicious recipes for dishes made of vegetables. Although in Italy we eat a lot of produce, I'd never considered eating plant-based foods exclusively. The support of this enthusiastic vegetarian community was infectious. I transitioned to a mostly plant-based, low-glycemic diet, but with the occasional pasta feast and seafood thrown in.

When I moved back to Italy and started cooking at home, I saw our family recipes through fresh eyes.

With my newfound zest for cooking, I reveled in the wide variety of interesting and natural ingredients I saw everywhere in Italy, such as sunchokes, chestnut flour, natural cold-pressed oils, and endless heirloom varieties of fruits and vegetables. I quickly went to work searching out traditional Italian recipes that were naturally vegetarian and adapting meat-based classics for my diet. Above all, I was adamant about developing meatless recipes that used only natural, whole foods, without tofu or processed meat substitutes.

I hounded my mother and grandmother to learn their techniques for making pasta and bread. Most of these techniques were centuries old, and it was thrilling to be a part of the tradition of passing down knowledge from mother to daughter. I searched through old cookbooks looking for recipes with no meat in them, hoping to uncover old or forgotten treasures. I begged neighbors and friends for their secret family recipes and spent hours in the kitchen, experimenting with alternative flours, updating unhealthy techniques such as deep-frying, and keeping heavy, starchy ingredients like cream or potatoes for special occasions alone.

My vegetarian friends in New York would love these recipes, I thought. One day I picked up my camera and snapped pictures of the food I'd made, sending them to friends via e-mail. Their reaction was so enthusiastic, I started a blog, *Hortus Cuisine*, so I could share my recipes with those who wished to reduce their meat intake or just rediscover eating vegetables. I wanted to give back to the group that had changed my outlook on food, but I also wanted to show that Italian food was so much more than the ubiquitous dishes like fettucine Alfredo or eggplant Parmesan that most people thought represented "Italian" in the States. Although there are others writing about Italian food, many are either expats who have moved to Italy or Italians writing in Italian. I saw there was a place for an authentic Italian voice, writing in English, about Italian cuisine that was completely vegetable based.

Moving back to Italy made me fall in love with its traditions and flavors all over again. My kitchen became my alchemist's laboratory as I learned about and experimented with ancient grains, indigenous varieties of legumes, and vegetables and fruit from our garden. I began to understand what it really means to eat to nourish the body, and I became so inspired to create new recipes with plant-based ingredients.

And so I sit at my wooden desk, looking out over my family's fields, and write about vegetarian food and work to develop satisfying and delicious recipes everyone will love. It's the marrying of traditional techniques and dishes with a new, modern focus on healthy ingredients that lies at the heart of my new plant-based cooking. New York City gave me a new perspective to share the flavors I love most from our countryside with the world.

THE NATURALLY VEGETARIAN MEDITERRANEAN PANTRY

To build your pantry, you don't need to buy a lot of exotic or expensive ingredients, but you'll want to choose your staples with care. The quality of the ingredients makes a big difference in these recipes, since the preparations are actually quite simple. This section will give you essential advice on how to shop for the ingredients you'll need—it will make your life easier and your recipes tastier!

OILS & VINEGARS

EXTRA-VIRGIN OLIVE OIL

Extra-virgin olive oil is one of the staples of an Italian pantry. Used for drizzling, finishing, and cooking, good-quality olive oil can transform a dish. Nowadays, most oils found in supermarkets are blends of olives from all over. Some small producers of Italian olive oil still produce extra-virgin olive oils from heirloom varieties or from a single variety of olive to obtain unique flavors.

There are a few things to keep in mind when choosing the right extra-virgin olive oil. First, look for oil that does not contain chemicals. Extra-virgin olive oil is the result of the first pressing of the olives, and this should be done using only mechanical methods of extraction. You should also look for oil that has been cold-pressed, meaning that the oil was obtained through pressing and grinding with millstones or modern steel presses. Check the label, as the method of extraction should always be indicated. Also, be sure to look at the date the oil was produced. Try to get the freshest possible and, at a minimum, look for oil that has been sitting for less than six months.

If you can, buy from a seller who will let you do a taste test. If possible, you want to find an olive oil that is piquant and leaves a tingling sensation in your mouth. When olive oils have been properly pressed and stored, they will have a high amount of polyphenols, which cause the tingling. Polyphenols are important antioxidants that help prevent free radicals from spreading in your body. Ultimately, the best olive oil is the one that tastes best to you. Extra-virgin olive oil can taste grassy, nutty, fruity, or even tomato-y. Because it has such a prominent flavor, try several and pick one you really like!

I recommend buying a less expensive olive oil for cooking and a higher-quality oil for dressings and finishing. Store the oil in a dark place and at a constant temperature. And finally, when you are cooking with the oil, don't let it get smoking hot because it will lose its nutrients.

OTHER COOKING OILS & FATS

I use cold-pressed sunflower oil for frying, as a substitute for butter in baked goods, occasionally as a substitute for olive oil in various recipes, or mixed with olive oil for jarred vegetables and *sott'oli*. Watch out for mass-produced vegetable oils—they are low-quality and chemically processed, so always read the labels and purchase organic or local oils when possible. Just like with olive oil, always choose oils that are mechanically cold-pressed and that contain no chemicals. Occasionally, I like to use virgin coconut oil in baked goods, or grass-fed organic local butter.

APPLE CIDER VINEGAR

Apple cider vinegar is an excellent base for salad dressings because of its mellow, fruity aftertaste and its alkalizing properties. Like most fermented foods, it's also a healthy power food: I've heard some old wisdom that you can boost your hair and nail health by drinking a tablespoon of apple cider vinegar diluted in warm water with a teaspoon of honey first thing in the morning. It can't hurt to try it!

WINE VINEGAR (RED & WHITE)

When my great-grandparents made wine, they would set some aside to make red wine vinegar. The jars of red wine were left to age in the cellar and their strong, almost pungent smell became stronger as the vinegar aged. When we served it at dinner, the scent was so strong that I could barely stand to sit at the table. But good wine vinegars are like that: with a kick, yet delicate and intensely flavorful. Red wine vinegar is perfect for reducing sauces and pan juices, while white wine vinegar, which is less sharp, makes a perfect addition to salad dressings.

BALSAMIC VINEGAR

Ideally, balsamic vinegar should be made with cooked-down, fermented wine must and nothing else. But that is a long and expensive process, so most balsamic vinegars also contain wine vinegar. Some cheap vinegars also contain caramel coloring and preservatives. Avoid those, and if you cannot invest in balsamic vinegar *Tradizionale di Modena* (see opposite), source balsamic vinegars that only list wine must and wine vinegar as ingredients. Balsamic vinegar should be a rich, dense black. If it looks watery, it is low-

quality and is best left on the shelf. You can also cook down regular balsamic vinegar yourself and make a Sweet Balsamic Glaze or a Savory Balsamic Glaze (see Sweet and Savory Balsamic Reductions and Glaze on page 50).

ACETO TRADIZIONALE DI MODENA

Aceto Tradizionale di Modena is a special kind of vinegar worth investing in. Produced in Modena and its provinces, it's made exclusively with cooked-down wine must alone, and aged for twelve to twenty-four years in wooden barrels. As the vinegar ages, it naturally reduces and becomes sweeter, and is put in smaller and smaller barrels until it reaches an intensely flavorful, slightly tart, fruity sweetness. The flavor changes depending on the kind of wood used for the barrels. *Aceto Balsamico Tradizionale* is very expensive, but just a few drops are enough to add its special flavor to foods ranging from fruit salads, gelato, pastas with pumpkin, to plain aged cheese.

GRAINS & LEGUMES

BEANS

Beans are one of the ingredients most rooted in Italian food traditions. The most common varieties are cannellini, white and buttery and perfect for salads and soups; borlotti (also known as cranberry beans due to their red stripes when raw), used for long cooking and stews; and red kidney beans, which have a sweet edge and are great in salads and in creamy soups. We also use pinto beans, black-eyed peas, lima beans, chickpeas, and several other regional subvarieties.

When cooking dried beans, always soak them for at least twenty-four hours. This not only reduces the cooking time but rids the beans of phytates, which prevent the absorption of important nutrients such as iron and calcium. Always discard the soaking water and, if possible, change it one or two times during the soaking process. When cooking, add a teaspoon of baking soda to make the skins softer and easier to digest or remove. Avoid adding salt, which toughens the skins.

LENTILS

Lentils are also a staple in Italian tradition, especially in the central regions around the Apennine Mountain region. Though traditional recipes use lentils for thick stews or soups, they are also lovely in salads. The most common varieties are large and small green (French) lentils, which tend to hold together well—perfect for salads—and regular brown lentils, which work well in all recipes. I love the Italian brown lentil variety called *castelluccio* or *colfiorito*, which is indigenous to Umbria and has an al dente texture that can stand longer cooking and a delicious nutty taste.

OTHER LEGUMES

Fava beans, and split green and yellow peas are also key ingredients in Italian cuisine—especially in stews and pasta dishes. Chickpeas are also often prepared on their own, simply stir-fried with olive oil, garlic, rosemary, and

Are canned legumes bad?

While dried or fresh beans do provide a better texture, I find myself using canned legumes every now and then. Look for salt-free and preservative-free options and thoroughly rinse the legumes before using. If you can, choose organic—they have better texture and flavor.

cherry tomatoes, and enjoyed cold in the warmer months. These legumes need a full twenty-four-hour soaking and have a longer cooking time than other legumes, but they are incredibly delicious and full of beneficial nutrients.

FARRO

Farro (*Triticum monococcum*) is the glorious king of all Italian grains. Widely used in Tuscany, Umbria, and the central regions of Italy, farro is the great-grandfather of all ancient grains and the first to be cultivated in the Fertile Crescent. It is high in protein and low in gluten, and is the most wonderful grain to use for soups, stews, and salads. Farro comes either unhulled (whole) or pearled. Pearled farro requires less soaking and has a shorter cooking time, but it contains fewer nutrients and less fiber. If you cannot find Italian farro, you can substitute spelt (*Triticum spelta*), its close cousin. Spelt is larger than Italian farro but very, very similar in taste and texture.

BARLEY (ORZO)

Barley, with its fat grain and chewy texture, is used just like farro but makes an even stronger statement in matters of mouthfeel. Like farro, barley comes both unhulled and pearled: unhulled barley should be soaked overnight, while pearled barley can be cooked after just an hour of soaking. Barley releases a lot of starch as it cooks, making it perfect for risotto-like preparations.

BUCKWHEAT

Buckwheat, a gluten-free, pyramid-shaped seed, is mostly used in the northernmost regions of

Italy, where the scenery is lined with the majestic Alps and Germany feels closer than the rest of Italy. Traditionally, it is used in soups and baked stews, and in flour form for baking bread and cakes. Buckwheat has a slightly smoky taste that makes it a perfect complement to bold flavors such as porcini, truffle, spices, or seasoned cheeses.

MILLET

The first time my family saw me eating millet, they teased me that I was eating bird feed. And this is what millet still means to most Italian farmers: it's a food for the poorest people, and perfect for feeding children and hens. To me, millet is delicious. It has a light taste, and what's more, millet's high concentration of B vitamins and minerals—especially zinc—makes it a wonderful hair- and nail-health booster.

POLENTA

Polenta, a food traditional to the regions of Veneto, Tuscany, and all of northern Italy, is made out of ground corn and is incredibly versatile. It comes in many varieties and flavors: for example, whole-grain polenta is made by coarsely grinding dried corn; polenta *taragna* is mixed with ground buckwheat; and white polenta is a special variety mostly used in Venice. You can cook it until it's creamy like a pudding, or make it thicker and allow it to set, then cut it into slices and eat it as is or grill it. Polenta is a quintessential winter food and can be topped with sauces in the same way as pasta—in fact, any pasta sauce in this book makes a great polenta topping. Grilled polenta is best for the warmer months. Choose whole corn Italian polenta, and look for the kind that has some dark speckles: coarse, speckled polenta is less processed and more delicious!

FLOURS & STARCHES

WHOLE-WHEAT FLOUR

I am a strong believer in using whole grains for everything, including flour. Except for special occasions, white flour doesn't find its way into my kitchen very often. White commercial flours are mass-produced, stripped of their nutrients, and often come from wheat of dubious quality. The lower the quality of the wheat, the more negatively it will affect the quality of things you make with it. I have seen homemade pasta turn out disastrously because of bad flours. Even many whole-wheat flours are just processed white flours to which only part of the bran has been added back. Therefore, if you can, buy your flours from a local mill or try to source stone-milled flours. If you can't get local flours, buy organic. This book contains some recipes for the holidays that call for white flours, but using whole-wheat flour alone produces good results as well, especially in preparations like pasta—so long as the flour is fresh.

SEMOLINA FLOUR

Semolina is flour made out of durum wheat. It has a yellowish color and coarse texture. It is traditionally used in southern Italy to make bread (in particular, Pugliese bread), focaccia, Sicilian couscous, Sardinian fregula, and some special kinds of rustic cakes and puddings. But the reason why all of Italy loves semolina is because it makes great pasta. Substitute semolina for a portion of regular flour (10 to 30 percent) when making savory baked goods to give them a chewy, more rustic feel. For pastas, you can use half semolina flour and half regular flour in your dough for a rich flavor and texture. Or try an all-semolina dough for something unique. The semolina flour usually sold in the United States comes from the Mediterranean area, but if you find Italian flour or a semolina flour that has been produced near you, go for that.

SPELT OR FARRO FLOUR

Because of its slightly sweet, pleasantly nutty taste and its ability to rise well, spelt flour is great for baking—especially breads, sweets, and cakes. Surprisingly, spelt flour is actually lower in gluten than wheat flour, but it contains more nutrients, so it is an overall healthier choice. Just like wheat flour, spelt and farro flour come in both white and whole form.

WHOLE RYE FLOUR

Rye flour has the lowest glycemic index, lowest gluten content (along with oat flour), and lowest caloric density of all flours. It is used especially in northern Italy for making bread and savory baked goods. It's also sometimes added to wheat flour to make pasta.

CHICKPEA FLOUR

Flour made out of chickpeas is the main ingredient to make a sort of Italian thick chickpea crepe called *farinata* or *cecina* that people enjoy in Liguria, Tuscany, and Sicily (find my Chickpea "Frittata" with Red Onions recipe on page 64). Chickpea flour is great for making crepes and savory pancakes, and for binding vegetarian meatballs and croquettes to make them gluten-free.

CHESTNUT FLOUR

Chestnut flour, with its smoky, nutty taste, is a wonderful addition to bread and pasta. In Liguria and Tuscany, there is a tradition of using chestnut flour to make pasta and then dressing it with other woodsy fall and winter flavors such as mushrooms, truffle, squash, sage, or rosemary. Chestnut flour is also used to make sweets and is often paired with honey and ricotta.

POTATO STARCH

Potato starch is good for achieving a fluffier, crumblier consistency in baked goods. Adding a small amount to recipes that call for whole flours will make your baked goods lighter, which is especially helpful in vegan baking.

RICE

ITALIAN RICE

Italian rice for risotto comes in four main varieties:

- ORIGINARIO, which is the starchiest and fastest cooking, and is used for arancini and rice cakes.

- SEMIFINO, which has short and plump grains and is the best for making risotto. One semifino variety is Vialone Nano, a kind of rice cultivated in Veneto that is the quintessential risotto rice: its pearly, plump grains are extremely starchy, which bonds with the cooking liquid and produces the creamiest, silkiest risottos.

- FINO, which holds up to slow cooking best and is mostly used for salads and soups.

- SUPERFINO, which includes the varieties Carnaroli and Arborio, the varieties most commonly used for making risotto.

BROWN & SPECIAL RICES

Italian rices have long been only available as white rices, but they are starting to make an appearance in brown form. Even though brown rice will not produce as creamy a risotto as regular white rice, it is a far healthier option and especially good for soupy risottos (*all'onda*, as Italians would call it).

Chickpea "Frittata"
with Red Onions, page 64

How to shop for good pasta

When shopping for dry pasta, look for pasta that is pale white and has a slight starch coating on the surface. Good-quality pasta usually comes in a see-through package. It will have ridged, uneven edges, and a very coarse texture, which helps the pasta cling to the sauce better. The coating of starch helps make the sauce creamier. Avoid pasta that looks rubbery, plasticky, or yellow.

As for egg pasta, make sure it does not contain any ingredients other than flour, eggs, and water. Try to buy it fresh rather than dried if you can, as it will have a better texture and taste.

Whole-wheat pasta is, of course, the healthiest choice, but it is not always easy to find tasty whole-wheat pasta. Follow the rules for shopping for white pasta—whole-wheat pasta should not look plastic-like, but rough and starchy. If the package says the pasta was slow dried and you can see a thin layer of dusty starch coating it, you can almost certainly trust it is good—white or whole-wheat pastas alike.

Store any opened pasta in an airtight container.

Brown and special varieties of rice are also good for salads. Aside from the Italian varieties I mentioned, I like to use *riso venere* (black rice) and red rice both for their pleasant, nutty flavor and for the minerals and vitamins they provide. Plus, the bran gives them some healthy fiber.

DRY PASTA

Dry pasta comes in a variety of shapes, and they are all delicious in their own way. There are a set of unwritten rules that Italians unconsciously use to pair the right pasta with the perfect sauce, since they all absorb sauces differently. Any good pasta is great paired with a well-cooked sauce, but finding that ideal pairing makes a pasta dish even tastier.

SHORT SHAPES

Short and plump pastas such as shells, penne, fusilli, farfalle, gemelli, and rigatoni are versatile and can be used with any sauce. They are also great for pasta salads. "Holey" pastas such as shells are wonderful with creamy and chunky sauces or hearty sauces that get deliciously stuck in their crevices.

LONG SHAPES

Spaghetti, linguine, and angel hair are great with tomato sauces, pesto, or creamy sauces. Long-shaped pastas are not so good with chunky sauces, since the forkfuls become a little difficult to manage. Try pairing any long pasta with Pesto Ligure (page 40) or Tomato Pesto (page 42). Thicker cuts, such as bucatini and ziti, are especially great when baked or added to frittatas.

PASTA FOR SOUP

The smallest pasta shapes, such as ditali, orzo, and stelline, are a great addition to soups and stews. They are usually cooked along with the soup, so that the starch in the pasta thickens the soup and makes it richer.

SPECIAL SHAPES

Italy has many regional shapes: trofie, two-inch-long twisty strands from Liguria; orecchiette, round durum wheat nuggets from Puglia; gnocchi-like tiny cavatelli from Molise; garganelli and strozzapreti from Romagna . . . the tempting list goes on. These shapes are usually cooked with ingredients that are indigenous to the region they come from (for example, Ligurian trofie are usually dressed with pesto, while Apulian orecchiette are usually dressed with chili, rapini, and sun-dried tomatoes), but it is fun to come up with sauces to pair a unique pasta. Specially shaped pastas have a plump and al dente consistency that makes them perfect with any sauce.

For recipes, see page 53.

PASTA ALL'UOVO (EGG PASTA)

Pasta made with eggs tastes best when it's homemade, but if you're in a hurry, you can also buy it fresh or dried (fresh is ideal, if you can). Pastas such as ravioli, cappelletti, tortellini, pappardelle, tagliatelle, and tagliolini are all made with eggs and taste wonderful with creamy, rich sauces—much like long pasta. If you make your own, try experimenting with greens, beet juice, porcini mushrooms, truffle, or tomato paste to add color and depth of flavor.

For recipes, see page 53.

CHEESE

IS YOUR CHEESE VEGETARIAN?

Unfortunately, not all cheeses are created equal. You may be surprised to learn that many traditional Italian cheeses are usually made with animal rennet. For example, Parmigiano-Reggiano, which is a gorgeous cheese of the highest quality produced in Emilia, must be produced with animal rennet because of Italian regulations. Parmigiano belongs to the DOP products category (*Denominazione di Origine Protetta*, "Protected Designation of Origin"), a seal of quality that can only be applied to products coming from a specific territory made with traditional methods. In fact, all certified Italian cheeses are made using animal rennet. Grana Padano, on the other hand, is a seasoned cheese produced in the Padan Plain area that bears the DOP seal as well, but it is generally easier to imitate for local farmers, who sometimes choose to produce it with vegetarian rennet. Many farmers produce Grana and, even though it cannot bear the DOP seal, they can still call it Grana as long as it is produced in the Padan area.

These days, more and more producers are choosing vegetarian rennet to make their cheeses. Read the labels or, if you can source your cheese from a local producer or specialty shop, ask how it was made. Another issue to consider is whether the cheese was made with milk from grass-fed cows, which produces a higher-quality product.

I am not a strict vegetarian, so I use Parmigiano-Reggiano and other DOP cheeses occasionally. Throughout the book, I use Parmigiano, Grana Padano, or pecorino cheeses, as well as fresh cheeses made with vegetarian rennet. If you are okay with using cheeses made with animal rennet, Italian Parmigiano that has been seasoned for twenty-four to thirty-two months is the best way to go, and is now quite easy to find in supermarkets and specialty stores worldwide. Cheese is a special-occasion food for me, so when I use it in my recipes, it must be the best I can afford!

Blue Cheese Pizza with
Radicchio & Balsamic Glaze,
page 118

HARD CHEESES

Hard cheeses are perfect for finishing pasta dishes, as a topping for casseroles, or as an addition to veggie burgers and meatballs and frittatas. When you shop for cheese, always ask where it comes from and how it was made. Store hard cheeses in the fridge, well wrapped in wax paper. If the cheese develops mold, it is only an indication that it is high-quality and has no chemicals or preservatives. Cut the mold off and you are good to go.

SOFT FRESH CHEESES

Mozzarella, burrata, ricotta, and robiola are just a few of the many Italian fresh cheeses available in the international market. Although you can find original fresh cheeses exported directly from Italy, many places outside of Italy offer fresh cheese, often made in-house and in small batches, by local supermarkets or specialty food stores. Most fresh cheeses are now made with vegetarian rennet. Keep them in the fridge and consume within three days.

CANNED GOODS

VEGETABLES PRESERVED IN OLIVE OIL

Artichokes, tomatoes, olives, eggplants, onions, and many other vegetables preserved in olive oil are essential for assembling antipasti platters, dips, spreads, and pesto. They can also be used to add an extra kick to pasta dishes or salads. Vegetables preserved in olive oil are often flavored with Mediterranean herbs or spices, and if you can find some preserved in quality olive oil, you can save the oil for cooking. Sun-dried tomatoes preserved in oil are my favorite and I use them quite a bit throughout this book. Read the label and make sure they are preserved in pure olive oil, or, if mixed with vegetable oils, make

sure the oil was not chemically processed. The price is going to be a little higher, but it is well worth it!

TOMATOES: PASSATA, WHOLE CANNED, PASTE

What would an Italian kitchen be without tomatoes? We use tomatoes in different forms, as I describe below. When shopping for these quintessential tomato staples, choose products that contain no salt or preservatives. They should only contain tomatoes. If you can, choose organic. Check the geographical origin of the tomatoes, and make sure they come from areas known for quality production (such as Italy or California). The best canned tomato goods are made with San Marzano, a kind of oblong, juicy tomato grown in southern Italy.

Tomato Passata

Tomato passata is perfect for making tomato pasta sauce (find the recipe, Tomato Sauce, on page 33) is nothing more than blanched tomatoes blended to a smooth puree, whereas Italian canned tomatoes are pretty much the same but left whole. Check the recipe for making your own Tomato Passata on page 237.

Whole Canned Tomatoes

You can find whole regular canned tomatoes or canned cherry tomatoes. I prefer the latter, as they tend to be a little tastier, but choose whatever is available. You can cut up whole canned tomatoes; they are perfect to coarsely cut up and add to chunky soups or Fall Tuscan Minestrone with Farro & Lots of Veggies (page 67), or use them to make a chunkier rather than smooth Spring Ragù Sauce (page 39). They will break up as they cook. Canned cherry tomatoes are also great for quick pasta sauces, like the Tomato Sauce on page 33.

Tomato Paste

Unlike passata, tomato paste is a super-concentrated tomato that can be used in sauces that need a hint of tomato flavor. It's best sautéed in oil early in a recipe so that it can fully release its flavor. Tomato paste should never be added later in a recipe, or it will not dissolve properly (for example, it will not dissolve in a liquid if added later).

OLIVES

Italian olives come in many forms: in brine, in olive oil, plain or *conciate*—pickled with spices and herbs. Green olives, such as large, fat Cerignola olives, are wonderful on their own or in simple salads, while black olives work well for cooking. I prefer the little black Ligurian Taggiasca olives. Often sold dressed in olive oil and maybe some herbs, their mild, round taste makes them perfect for any dish.

CAPERS

Capers are the buds of the flower of the caper plant, which grows on low, crawling bushes and is mostly cultivated in Sicily. They are preserved either in salt or in a vinegary brine. Capers have a strong, unique flavor that makes a statement in pastas, condiments, and marinades, and in all sorts of dishes of Mediterranean inspiration. Whether they are preserved in salt or vinegar, always rinse them well before using.

TRUFFLE PASTE

You can find truffle paste made with pure truffle, or, for a cheaper option, look for a truffle and porcini mix. Both are really tasty, and just a teaspoon in a fall or winter pasta sauce will be enough to fill your kitchen with its intoxicating aroma. You can also use truffle paste in pasta dough, polenta, and sauces that don't involve tomatoes, or use it on bruschetta for a mushroom-based spread.

Truffle paste also pairs especially well with cheeses, peas, and winter squash. When adding to your preparations, always add it at the end of the cooking process so it retains the most flavor. When used in pasta sauces, add a teaspoon or two when the sauce is done before tossing the sauce with the pasta. Try it spread in a very thin layer on the base of a pizza before adding the other toppings and then bake the pizza.

DRY GOODS

SALT

I avoid regular refined table salt in cooking and stick with unrefined sea salt. There are so many varieties of salt; some of my favorites are Celtic salts, namely sel gris (gray salt) and fleur de sel (flower of salts), which are natural sea salts harvested in northern France and England. Both are wonderful for both cooking and finishing. Some salts are both delicious and naturally rich in minerals: Hawaiian salt, with its reddish hue, is rich in iron; black salt usually contains active carbon and has an earthy flavor; and Himalayan salt gets its pinkish hue from mineral deposits it has collected over the thousands of years it's been underground. Flavored salts, such as truffle salt, lemon salt, smoked salt, and herb salt, are also a fun way to finish many a vegetarian dish and create a "wow" effect. You can now find flavored salts in most supermarkets.

PEPPER & SPICES

Pepper, both black and white, are essential to Italian cooking. It is best to buy whole peppercorns and grind them as needed because ground pepper tends to get spicier and lose its more subtle flavor as it sits. White pepper is milder, but black pepper is my go-to pepper and the one I use most in this book.

The other spices that Italians use regularly are coriander seeds for savory dishes and vanilla beans for sweet preparations. Even though vanilla extract is not used in Italy, I use it in many of the recipes in this book.

HERBS

In the cold season, the Italian herb pantry consists of rosemary, sage, thyme, and bay leaves. In summer, we use basil, parsley, mint, marjoram, and oregano. To preserve fresh herbs, chop them finely, then freeze them in plastic jars or ziplock bags and pull them out as needed.

If you can find them, buy whole branches of dried herbs, such as oregano or rosemary. If you can only find pre-ground dried herbs, do not buy large amounts, as the flavor tends to get lost easily. Once open, store them in airtight jars to minimize the loss of their aroma.

RED PEPPER FLAKES (OR WHOLE DRIED ITALIAN CHILI PEPPERS)

Italian pepper flakes are not as spicy as Indian or Asian varieties, but they do provide a nice kick to tomato-based and garlic-based pasta sauces, such as puttanesca or marinara. To use red pepper flakes, add them as you heat olive oil to start any vegetable sauté or sauce. Store the whole peppers or flakes in a tightly sealed glass jar to preserve their freshness and spiciness. Remember to wash your hands after handling!

DRIED PORCINI MUSHROOMS

Fresh porcini mushrooms can be hard to find, so you can use dried porcini mushrooms to add their rich flavor to any dish. Just a few slivers of dried porcini can transform pastas, risotto and stews. To prepare dried porcinis, rehydrate them in hot water for a minimum of thirty minutes (you can also soak them overnight). Do not discard the soaking water! Filter it with a fine-mesh strainer or a piece of cheesecloth (or even just a paper towel) to get rid of the dirt and deposits, and add it to whatever preparation in which you will be using the dried porcini. For example, swap the porcini liquid for some of the stock when making risotto, or add it to a mushroom-based pasta sauce. You can also use it when making soups and braises.

FINELY GROUND BREAD CRUMBS

Bread crumbs are used in many traditional dishes and as a topping for vegetables and casseroles. You can make your own out of stale whole-wheat or rye bread by grating it on a fine cheese grater or using a food processor or blender. Store the bread crumbs in an airtight container.

SUGAR

I love to use dark brown sugar in my baking. For special occasions, I like to make my own powdered sugar by processing some organic brown cane sugar in a powerful blender or coffee grinder.

You can add vanilla beans to the sugar you use for baking, and use the resulting vanilla-flavored sugar for any dessert recipe. They will lend their delicious scent!

HONEY

Italy has so many kinds of honey, all with their own distinctive properties and flavor. The easiest to find worldwide is probably acacia honey, a mild, delicate, intensely flowery kind of honey that I use most in my recipes—I love the ever-so-slight tingling sensation it leaves in the back of your throat. Millefiori honey, which usually crystallizes and tastes richer and more caramel-like when compared to acacia, is also a good choice for any kind of dessert. I source my honey directly from beekeepers, so it is always unheated/raw, but store-bought works just as well for the recipes in this book.

BEFORE YOU BEGIN
Notes on the Recipes

SALT: The salt I use in these recipes is either unrefined sea salt or kosher salt.

PEPPER: Unless otherwise indicated, I use freshly ground black pepper. I have a pepper mill and prefer to use that, as ground pepper left to sit tends to change flavor and get spicier.

ONIONS, GARLIC & VEGETABLES: Wash and dry all your vegetables thoroughly before getting started with any recipe. The onions and garlic are always peeled before cutting, unless otherwise specified.

EGGS: I use large eggs, weighing about 2 ounces (55–60 grams) each. I recommend buying fresh, free-range organic eggs, from a small local farm if possible. Use special care if you are cooking anything that involves raw or partially cooked eggs. When beating egg whites, make sure to do so with perfectly clean bowls and whisks, as any trace of fat might compromise the final result. Choose stainless-steel or glass bowls for best results.

STOCK: Homemade always tastes best, but if you cannot make stock at home, use a good-quality, good-tasting, sodium-free store-bought stock.

SUGAR: I only use dark or light brown organic sugar. I prefer it over white granulated sugar, unless it is specifically needed for a recipe. The ingredients lists indicate the kind of sugar you'll need for each recipe.

FLOUR: I buy stone-milled flour from a local mill, and I always use stone-milled flour, whether I need white or whole wheat. Of course, not everyone has a mill close to home. If you cannot purchase stone-milled whole-wheat flour, buy organic whole-wheat flour. Store-bought whole-wheat flour is usually not as fine as stone-milled, so you might want to process it in a high-speed blender or a coffee grinder before using for best results.

PASTA: All the recipes will work well with store-bought fresh pasta if you cannot make fresh pasta yourself. When possible, choose artisanal or handmade pasta from a specialty shop.

CHEESE: I prefer Parmigiano, pecorino, and Grana Padano—the latter two can be found made with vegetarian rennet. Try to buy all of your cheese locally, if possible, or be sure that it's good-quality.

BUTTER: I do not use much butter when I'm cooking, but when I do, I want it to be the best possible quality. I prefer butter made from organic milk from grass-fed cows. If you live near a farmer or a producer who produces butter this way, buy it directly from them (I try to buy all my dairy products locally from farms using grass-fed cows). I always use unsalted butter.

Not all ovens are created the same, so cooking time may vary, sometimes significantly. Start keeping a close eye on what you are baking at least ten minutes before the cooking time indicated in the recipe is up.

When you see the indication to "half cover" a pot, put on the lid but keep it slightly ajar, so that some steam can escape.

The oven I use is a standard oven. Refer to your manufacturer's manual for instructions on your specific oven for best results.

The pans and skillets used are always nonstick, unless otherwise specified.

Finally, we all have our own preferences, so taste and sniff as you are cooking. You'll learn to make these recipes your own and adjust them to your liking. Most important, have fun!

Spring Ragù Sauce,
page 39

BASIC RECIPES

These staples have been used in my household for generations—my kitchen just could not operate without them. You can probably find all of these ready to buy in a store, but I am so used to making these recipes at home that I am sure my cooking would lack that homemade flavor if I did not make them myself. Learn these recipes once, and repeat them ad libitum.

Vegetable Stock • Tomato Sauce • Simple Marinara Sauce • Béchamel Sauce
Vegetarian "Bolognese" Sauce • Spring Ragù Sauce • Pesto Ligure • Tomato Pesto
Tapenade (Pesto di Olive) • Ligurian Pesto, Tomato Pesto, or Tapenade Dressing
Classic Bruschetta • Quick Pizza • Crumb Topping "Alla Romagnola" • Bread Crumbs
Sweet & Savory Balsamic Reductions & Glaze • Classic Vanilla Custard

THIS IS A SIMPLE STOCK for soups, stews, risottos, and more. I prefer to keep the salt content low, so that I can add salt to taste when I use it in a dish. If you are not using the stock all at once, you can easily divide it into storage containers and freeze, then thaw it whenever you need.

VEGETABLE STOCK

MAKES 12 CUPS (3 LITERS)

2 bay leaves, whole

1 garlic clove, whole

1 teaspoon peppercorns

1 small leek (substitute 1 more medium onion if you don't have a leek), well cleaned and coarsely chopped

2 medium carrots, coarsely chopped

1 medium onion, coarsely chopped

1 celery stalk, with its leaves if possible, coarsely chopped

8 cherry tomatoes, coarsely chopped (optional)

1 medium zucchini, coarsely chopped

1 small potato, coarsely chopped

6 or 7 sprigs fresh flat-leaf parsley

1 teaspoon salt

12 cups (3 l) water

1. Put the bay leaves, garlic clove, and peppercorns in a sachet or in a tea ball filter.

2. Put the remaining ingredients in a large pot, add the sachet, cover, and bring to a boil. Reduce the heat to keep your stock simmering steadily. Cover and cook for 1½ hours. Filter the stock. Now it is ready to use, or you can divide it into jars and freeze.

TIP: Do not throw out the vegetables! You can make *passato di verdura*—a simple cream of vegetables—with them. After you fish out the bay leaves, peppercorns, and garlic and filter the stock, transfer the boiled vegetables to a blender with enough stock to make a creamy soup (4 to 6 cups, depending on how thick you like it). Adjust the salt and pepper to taste. If you want to keep all the stock for another dish or store it instead, you can blend the vegetables with water and add a little extra salt. Finish with a drizzle of extra-virgin olive oil and a teaspoon or two of grated Grana.

OUR CLASSIC, SIMPLE HOMEMADE TOMATO SAUCE involves no garlic. In my home, and in the homes of many people I know, garlic is used to make marinara, which is different from this classic tomato sauce (see my recipe for Simple Marinara Sauce on page 34). You can, of course, sauté a garlic clove with the onion and celery in the first step if you so fancy.

This recipe is perfect made with tomato passata, but if all you have on hand are whole canned tomatoes, they will work just as well—just blend the sauce when it is ready. Try all versions, and pick your favorite!

TOMATO SAUCE

MAKES ABOUT 2 CUPS (500 ML)

2 tablespoons olive oil

1 small onion, finely chopped

½ small carrot, finely chopped

One 2-inch (5 cm) piece of celery, finely chopped

2 cups (16 oz/500 ml) packed chopped fresh or canned tomatoes, or 2 cups (500 ml) Tomato Passata (page 237)

1 cup (250 ml) water

8 to 10 fresh basil leaves, plus 3 fresh basil leaves, finely chopped, for finishing

1 teaspoon salt

¼ teaspoon pepper

1. Heat the olive oil in a medium pot over medium-high heat and add the onion, carrot, and celery. Sauté for 2 to 3 minutes, until the onion is translucent. Add the tomatoes and water. Tear the 8 to 10 fresh basil leaves and add, then add the salt and pepper and stir well. Reduce the heat to the low and let the sauce simmer, half-covered, for 50 minutes to 1 hour, stirring every now and then to make sure it is not sticking to the pot.

2. Once the sauce is ready, stir in the finely chopped basil. At this point, you can decide to leave it a bit chunky—you will taste the bits of onion and carrot—or you can blend it until smooth in a blender or directly in the pot using an immersion blender.

3. You can portion the sauce into jars and freeze it for later use.

WHILE OTHER TOMATO SAUCES NEED TO COOK FOR A LONG TIME, this quick ten-minute sauce can be made to accompany any last-minute bruschetta or pasta. You can also use it as a pizza sauce. The olive oil in this recipe makes it quite rich, but if you prefer, you can make a delicious marinara with half the oil.

SIMPLE MARINARA SAUCE

MAKES 1 CUP (250 ML)

¼ cup (60 ml) olive oil

3 garlic cloves, finely minced

2 tablespoons finely minced fresh parsley

1 cup (250 ml) tomato passata

½ teaspoon salt, plus more as needed

Pinch of pepper, plus more as needed

3 fresh basil leaves

½ teaspoon dried oregano, if you like it

Heat the olive oil in a medium pot on medium-high heat and add the garlic and parsley. Sauté until the garlic and parsley release their aroma, about 3 minutes. Add the tomato passata, salt, and pepper. Tear the basil leaves and add. Stir well, and let the sauce simmer over medium-low heat for about 10 minutes, until the oil rises to the surface. Stir every few minutes to make sure the sauce does not stick to the pot. Stir in the oregano if you like, and add salt and pepper to taste.

THE RULE OF THUMB for making béchamel sauce is 50 grams fat, 50 grams flour, and 500 milliliters liquid, which converts to approximately 4 tablespoons fat, ⅓ cup flour, and 2 cups liquid. For the vegan version, try unsweetened soy milk or almond milk. I do not recommend using rice milk, which is too watery and too sweet, or any other milk that is low in fat. I love the taste of olive oil in this vegan béchamel sauce, but feel free to use a more neutral oil instead, such as a good organic sunflower oil, if you prefer a lighter flavor.

BÉCHAMEL SAUCE

....
MAKES ABOUT 2 CUPS (500 ML)
....

4 tablespoons (1.7 oz/50 g) butter

⅓ cup (1.7 oz/50 g) flour

2 or 3 gratings of nutmeg

½ teaspoon salt, plus more as needed

Pinch of pepper

2 cups (500 ml) warm full-fat milk

Melt the butter in a small pot over medium-high heat. Remove from the heat and stir in the flour. Whisk with a balloon whisk until a paste forms. Add the nutmeg, salt, and pepper. Place the pot over medium-high heat again and, as you keep whisking slowly, add the warm milk in a stream. You will need to constantly whisk the béchamel sauce as it cooks—do not leave it alone, as it sticks very easily. Shortly after it starts steaming, about 3 minutes, the béchamel sauce will start to thicken. Whisk more vigorously, until the béchamel sauce turns creamy. Do not overcook—the béchamel sauce will thicken further as it cools. Remove the pot from the heat as soon as the béchamel sauce turns creamy and keep whisking for 1 minute more. Taste and adjust the salt and nutmeg as you wish. If you let the sauce sit until it has completely cooled and thickened too much, just add a couple of tablespoons of warm milk, heat it up again, and stir it until smooth.

FOR A VEGAN VARIATION: Use ¼ cup (60 ml) olive oil instead of the butter and unsweetened almond milk instead of regular milk. Stir in 1 tablespoon nutritional yeast as soon as the sauce is removed from the heat and whisk it in well.

BOLOGNESE IS A KEY SAUCE IN ITALIAN COOKING, especially in the traditional cuisine of Emilia-Romagna, and was a staple of our Sunday meals when I was growing up. Bolognese is also one of the most meat-and-fat-heavy preparations in Italian cuisine, so I set out to make a lighter, vegetarian version. This "mock Bolognese" is a healthier option, and absolutely tasty in its own right. I did "cheat" a bit and got out of my Italian comfort zone when I created this recipe. You'll see it calls for soy sauce and miso paste to ramp up the umami flavor (if someone asks, tell them an Italian said it was okay). Use this sauce as you would use regular Bolognese in pasta, lasagna, cannelloni, and so on. This recipe yields a small batch, but it easily doubles or triples. One note: The more finely you can chop the vegetables in this recipe, the better!

VEGETARIAN "BOLOGNESE" SAUCE

SERVES 4

6 tablespoons (90 ml) olive oil

1 medium onion, finely chopped

2 medium carrots, finely chopped

1 celery stalk with leaves attached, finely chopped

½ cup (125 ml) dry red wine

1 pound (450 g) button mushrooms, very finely chopped

2 tablespoons tomato paste

1 tablespoon soy sauce

1 bay leaf

1 heaping teaspoon miso paste

1½ cups (375 ml) tomato passata

½ cup (125 ml) almond milk or regular milk

½ cup (125 ml) water or Vegetable Stock (page 32)

1 tablespoon finely chopped fresh basil

1 tablespoon finely chopped fresh parsley

1 heaping teaspoon nutritional yeast

½ teaspoon salt, plus more as needed

Pinch of pepper

1. In a large pot, heat 4 tablespoons (60 ml) olive oil over medium heat. Add the onion, carrots, and celery and raise the heat to medium-high. Cook, stirring often, for about 5 minutes, until the vegetables are translucent. The vegetables will release water. Raise the heat to high and cook for 10 to 15 minutes, until all the water is gone and the oil is starting to render on the surface. Deglaze the pan with ¼ cup of the wine and cook until it is completely reduced. If some liquid remains, continue cooking and stirring until it evaporates.

2. In a separate pan, heat the remaining 2 tablespoons olive oil and add the mushrooms. Cook on high, stirring often, until the water released by the mushrooms has completely evaporated and the mushrooms start to brown. When the mushrooms start caramelizing on the bottom of the pan, deglaze the pan with the remaining ¼ cup (75 ml) wine and cook until the wine has completely evaporated. Add the tomato paste and soy sauce and stir until dissolved.

3. Scrape the mushrooms into the pot with the other vegetables and reduce the heat to medium. If the vegetables

recipe continues

release more water, raise the heat to high and cook until the water evaporates, then reduce the heat to medium.

4. Add the bay leaf, miso paste, tomato passata, almond milk, water, basil, parsley, nutritional yeast, salt, and pepper. Reduce the heat to low so that the Bolognese simmers slowly.

5. Cook, half-covered, until the sauce turns dense and creamy, about 1 hour. Stir every now and then to make sure it does not stick to the bottom. The sauce should be thick, just like regular Bolognese. If needed, cook for longer until you achieve the desired consistency. When done, discard the bay leaf.

6. Serve with any pasta. Also try using this recipe on the Pumpkin Gnocchi with Sage & Pumpkin Seed Pesto (page 80) or Ricotta Gnocchi with Saffron, Zucchini & Cherry Tomatoes (page 197) with a nice sprinkling of grated cheese.

THIS SAUCE IS WONDERFUL IN LASAGNA instead of a classic ragù, or poured over short, hollow pastas such as shells, fusilli, or orecchiette. It's a rich ragù sure to fill your kitchen with scents of Italian Easter, and it won't leave you missing the meat at all. You can also substitute it for the vegetarian Bolognese (page 36) in any recipe that calls for it.

SPRING RAGÙ SAUCE

SERVES 6 TO 8

6 tablespoons (90 ml) olive oil

1 small onion, finely chopped

One 4-inch piece of celery, finely chopped

1 small carrot, finely chopped

1 pound (450 g) asparagus, chopped in ¼-inch (5 mm) rounds

1 medium zucchini, cut in half and finely sliced

4 artichoke hearts, fresh or frozen, cleaned and trimmed if fresh (see Note), and finely sliced

½ cup (2.8 oz/80 g) peas

½ cup (125 ml) dry white wine

½ cup (125 ml) water or Vegetable Stock (page 32), plus more as needed

1 teaspoon salt, plus more as needed

½ teaspoon pepper, plus more as needed

Heat the olive oil in a large pot over medium-high heat and add the onion, celery, and carrot. Sauté for 3 to 4 minutes, until aromatic. Add the asparagus, zucchini, artichokes, and peas and sauté for 1 minute more to coat the vegetables evenly with oil. Deglaze with the white wine, stirring for about 5 minutes until it has reduced. Add the water, salt, and pepper and stir. Cook over low heat, half-covered, for about 40 minutes, until the vegetables are very tender and the water has reduced. If the water evaporates too quickly, add a little more. Uncover the pot, raise the heat to medium, and cook for about 5 minutes, until the sauce thickens. Adjust the salt and pepper to taste. Use right away, or transfer to jars and freeze.

NOTE: To clean and trim a fresh artichoke, first cut off the stalk. Remove the first two crowns of tough outer leaves, cut off the spiky top, and cut in half. If there is any fuzz in the heart of the artichoke, remove it with a spoon.

You can add the first inch (2.5 cm) of the stalk to the ragù: Cut off the end that was attached to the artichoke, peel it like you would an apple, and thinly slice it.

PESTO, WITH ITS BRILLIANT GREEN, is one of the prides and glories of the whole Boot. Born in Liguria in northwestern Italy, it is one of the most delicious ways to dress your pastas, but pesto also adds rich flavor to sandwiches and panini, bruschetta with chopped cherry tomatoes, pizzas . . . go wild with the possibilities! Make it using a mortar and pestle to preserve the whole flavor of fresh basil. If you do not have a mortar and pestle (or enough patience), it tastes delicious made in a food processor or blender, too.

PESTO LIGURE

MAKES ABOUT 1 CUP (250 ML)

1 garlic clove

½ teaspoon salt

3 to 5 walnuts, or 1 heaping tablespoon pine nuts

2 cups (1.7 oz/50 g) tightly packed fresh basil leaves

6 tablespoons (1 oz/30 g) grated pecorino cheese

2 tablespoons grated Grana cheese

½ cup (125 ml) extra-virgin olive oil

1. **In a mortar and pestle:** Crush the garlic and the salt together, then add the nuts. Grind it all together until it forms a paste, then add a third of the basil leaves. Pound in a circular motion, tearing the leaves so that they release their green liquid. Add another third of the basil and repeat. Add the cheeses and grind well, then add the last third of the basil leaves. Once the paste is mixed and uniform, slowly add the olive oil in a stream as you keep grinding. **In a food processor:** Add all of the ingredients and blend until smooth.

2. Pesto will keep well in the fridge for 5 to 6 days.

FOR A VEGAN VARIATION: Omit the cheese, add 2 more walnuts, and your pesto will be just as delicious. Optional, but nice: Add a tablespoon of nutritional yeast for a hint of cheesy flavor.

THIS PESTO FOLLOWS THE SAME CONCEPT AS LIGURIAN PESTO, but the recipe uses almonds instead of walnuts. I love adding ricotta. However, you can keep this dairy-free and still make an absolutely delicious pesto—the basil and sun-dried tomatoes are so rich in flavor, you will hardly need the cheese. A single whiff of this magical red paste will transport you instantly under the warm southern Italian sun.

TOMATO PESTO

MAKES ABOUT 1 CUP (250 ML)

5 cherry tomatoes

1 garlic clove, peeled

5 or 6 almonds, or 1 heaping tablespoon pine nuts

2 cups (1.7 oz/50 g) tightly packed fresh basil leaves

6 tablespoons (1 oz/30 g) grated pecorino cheese

⅓ cup (1.2 oz/36 g) sun-dried tomatoes preserved in olive oil

⅓ cup fresh (2.8 oz/80 g) ricotta cheese (optional)

⅓ cup (75 ml) extra-virgin olive oil

In a blender, place the cherry tomatoes, garlic, almonds, basil, pecorino, sun-dried tomatoes, and ricotta, if using. Blend until creamy. With the blender running, add the olive oil in a stream until your pesto is creamy. Store in a jar in the fridge for up to 3 days.

FOR A VEGAN VARIATION: Leave out the ricotta cheese and double the amount of nuts. The sun-dried tomatoes are so rich in flavor that this pesto does not necessarily need the cheese. Adjust the salt to taste. The vegan version will keep about a week in the fridge.

ALONG THE ROCKY COASTS OF LIGURIA, where the marine breeze caresses thousands of Taggiasca olive trees, tapenade (or olive pesto, if you prefer) is a common recipe that arrives from Provence. It's handy to have a jar of it in the fridge to add to bruschetta, sandwiches, and dressings, or to use whenever you need to add a kick of umami. Toss it into salads, plain steamed greens, or boiled potatoes. It will keep in the fridge for about ten days.

TAPENADE (PESTO DI OLIVE)

....

MAKES ½ CUP (125 ML)

....

4.5 ounces (130 g) Marinated Olives (page 232)

1 large garlic clove

2 tablespoons capers, rinsed

8 fresh basil leaves

2 tablespoons chopped fresh parsley

1 tablespoon freshly-squeezed lemon juice

Salt (optional; see Tip)

6 to 7 tablespoons (90 to 105 ml) extra-virgin olive oil

In a food processor, place the olives, garlic, capers, basil, parsley, lemon juice, and salt, if using. Process until it forms a paste. With the processor running, add the olive oil in a stream until the ingredients are well blended. Store in a jar in the fridge for up to 10 days.

TIP: You can use your favorite store-bought pitted olives instead. Just keep in mind that the amount of salt you should add to tapenade largely depends on the olives you use. If you are using cured or marinated olives, you will not need to add any salt, whereas if you use plain olives, you might want to add ½ teaspoon. Taste, and adjust to your own liking.

LIGURIAN PESTO, TOMATO PESTO, OR TAPENADE DRESSING

....

You can add pesto to salad dressing to create a deeply flavorful, absolutely delicious dressing. In a jar, make a classic dressing with ½ cup (125 ml) extra-virgin olive oil; ¼ cup (60 ml) white wine vinegar, balsamic or apple cider vinegar (or lemon juice); ¼ teaspoon salt; and 2 pinches of pepper. Add a tablespoon of pesto. Shake well and store in the fridge for up to 4 days.

WHO CAN RESIST THE HEAVENLY SMELL OF GARLIC AND OLIVE OIL brushed on a thick slice of toasted sourdough? I love bruschetta with soups, or as a side to scoop up sauces or cooked vegetables. You can also top bruschetta with raw tomatoes and basil, or any other ingredient you like.

CLASSIC BRUSCHETTA

SERVES AS MANY AS YOU LIKE

½-inch-thick (or thicker) slices whole-wheat bread or other whole-flour sourdough bread

1 garlic clove, halved

Extra-virgin olive oil

Salt

Preheat the oven to 400°F (205°C). Place the bread slices on a rimmed baking sheet and bake for about 5 minutes, until toasted. Rub each slice with garlic, and brush on liberal amounts of extra-virgin olive oil. Sprinkle a tiny bit of salt on top of the bruschetta and serve hot. Toppings are optional.

THIS IS A RECIPE MY FAMILY HAS BEEN MAKING FOR YEARS AND YEARS, and it never fails to please and delight. Far from the Italian pie you get in wood-fired oven pizzerias, it's most similar to an American "Sicilian" square slice. Every home in Italy has their own recipe for making it. You can bake the dough in rectangular baking pans and cut it into squares, or make a circular shape. It's also great for stuffed pizza pies or mini pizza buns. "Quick" means that it uses active dry yeast rather than sourdough, but you still need to set aside time to let the dough rise. You can leave it mostly unattended, but make sure to start it a few hours ahead. Use this dough for recipes such as Erbazzone Spelt Pizza Pie Stuffed with Wild Greens (page 162) and Blue Cheese Pizza with Radicchio and Balsamic Glaze (page 118).

QUICK PIZZA

SERVES 4 TO 6; MAKES TWO 13 × 9-INCH (33 × 22-CM) PIZZAS

2½ teaspoons (0.3 oz/10 g) active dry yeast, or 1 cube (0.9 oz/25 g) fresh yeast

1½ cup (375 ml) warm water

1 tablespoon extra-virgin olive oil, plus more for the pan

2½ cups (10.5 oz/300 g) whole-wheat flour

1⅔ cups (7 oz/200 g) bread flour

1 teaspoon salt

For the classic "Margherita" pizza topping:

Pizza Tomato Sauce (see page 48)

2 cups (16 oz/230 g) shredded mozzarella

Handful of fresh basil leaves

Extra-virgin olive oil, for drizzling

1. In a small bowl, dissolve the yeast in ½ cup (125 ml) of the warm water, then add the olive oil and whisk well. (Using a fork is the easiest way, especially if you are using fresh yeast—mashing it against the sides of the bowl helps.) In a large bowl, place the whole-wheat flour, bread flour, and salt and whisk to combine. Add the water and yeast mixture to the flours and mix with a fork to combine. Knead the dough for 10 minutes, in a stand mixer, in a bread machine, or with your hands. The dough will be quite stretchy and slightly sticky. Cover the bowl with plastic wrap and wrap a tea towel around it. Allow it to rise in a warm place with no drafts until it doubles in size, 1½ to 2 hours.

2. After the dough rises, scrape it from the bowl and turn it out onto a well-floured work surface. Knead for 5 minutes.

3. Grease two 9 × 13-inch (33 × 22 cm) baking pans with olive oil. Divide the dough in half and stretch it with your oiled hands into the pans.

4. Once the dough is stretched, let it proof, covered with tea towels, for about 1½ hours, or until doubled in size.

5. Preheat the oven to 475°F (250°C).

recipe continues

NOTE: If you use a circular pan or two pans that are not 9 × 13 inches (33 × 22 cm), keep in mind that once your dough is stretched into the pans, it will rise threefold during proofing and baking. For example, stretching the dough to ¼-inch (5 mm) thickness will yield a ¾-inch-thick (1.5 cm) pizza, while stretching it to ½-inch (1.2 cm) thickness will result in a thick and fluffy focaccia.

6. To make a classic Margherita pizza: Spread the Pizza Tomato Sauce evenly over the pizzas and bake for 15 minutes.

7. Take the pizza out and sprinkle with the mozzarella. Tear the basil leaves and scatter random pieces on top. Finish with a thin drizzle of olive oil. Bake for 10 minutes more, or until the edges are golden and slightly crispy.

PIZZA TOMATO SAUCE *Makes 2 cups (250 ml)*

2 cups (250 ml) tomato passata

1 teaspoon salt or more or less to taste

2 pinches of pepper

2 tablespoons olive oil

1 tablespoon rinsed and finely chopped capers

1 tablespoon dried oregano or more or less to taste

Combine all the ingredients in a medium bowl and mix well. You can prepare the sauce up to a day in advance and store it in the fridge.

WE USE THIS FLAVORFUL CRUMB TOPPING in many recipes in Romagna. To make it, you use a basic technique that is easy to master and you can use it in several dishes in this book.

CRUMB TOPPING "ALLA ROMAGNOLA"

....
MAKES ABOUT ¾ CUP (175 ML)
....

½ cup (1.8 oz/50 g) homemade whole-grain bread crumbs (see below)

¼ cup (50 ml) extra-virgin olive oil

3 large garlic cloves, finely chopped

¼ cup (a large handful) packed fresh parsley, finely chopped

1 teaspoon salt

1 teaspoon pepper

Combine the bread crumbs, olive oil, garlic, parsley, salt, and pepper in a medium bowl and mix well. For a more flavorful result, prepare the crumb topping the same day or a few hours before you need it. It can be stored in the fridge for about 3 days.

BREAD CRUMBS
....

To make your own bread crumbs, just save your leftover whole-grain bread until it is stale and has completely hardened. We keep ours in a fabric bag, and after about a week it is good to go. You can also keep it in a basket covered with a tea towel. Keep it in a dry place where it can breathe—whole-grain bread can easily develop mold.

When the bread is rock-hard, break it into smaller pieces (or cut it before it gets too hard) and process it in a blender or food processor until it becomes very fine bread crumbs. We like to grind ours to a polenta-like consistency, or even finer. If you want superfine crumbs, pass them through a sieve.

THESE THICK SYRUPS from the region of Emilia add a hint of classy, sharp sweetness when used as a topping for salads, raw or cooked vegetables, sautéed vegetables, cheeses, mushrooms, or pastas and risottos that involve cheese, pumpkin, or radicchio. Just drizzle liberal amounts and taste the wow effect. Try the sweet glaze variation drizzled over fresh fruit, ice cream (yes, really), or other creamy vanilla-flavored desserts.

SWEET & SAVORY BALSAMIC REDUCTIONS & GLAZE

....

MAKES ABOUT ½ CUP (125 ML)

....

1 cup (250 ml) good-quality balsamic vinegar

1 scant tablespoon (15 ml) honey or packed dark brown sugar

Savory:

1 clove

One ½-inch (1.5 cm) piece of cinnamon

2 juniper berries (can be skipped if you do not have any)

1 teaspoon herbs such as rosemary, thyme, or sage (optional)

Sweet:

One ½-inch piece of cinnamon

½ teaspoon vanilla extract, or one 1-inch piece of vanilla bean, seeds scraped

1. In a small saucepan over low heat, place the vinegar and either the savory flavorings or the sweet flavorings and combine. Bring to a slow simmer and boil down the mixture for about 15 minutes, or until it reduces by almost half, stirring every 5 minutes with a wooden spoon. At first, the reduction might still look very liquidy, but it will thicken as it cools, so it is important to not overcook it.

2. The reduction is best used right away but can be stored in a jar in the fridge for up to 2 days.

FOR A BALSAMIC GLAZE: Balsamic glaze is an extra-thick variation of a standard reduction. To make the glaze, bring your reduced vinegar to a slow simmer over low heat. Meanwhile, in a separate small bowl, mix 1 teaspoon potato starch in ¼ cup (50 ml) water (the starch will not actually dissolve). While stirring the vinegar with a wooden spoon, add the water-starch mixture a little at a time. Cook for 2 minutes after you've added all the starch and remove the pan from the heat. Stir for 1 minute more and let cool.

THIS IS A CLASSIC ITALIAN-STYLE CUSTARD CREAM we have always enjoyed in my family. I love this recipe as is, but if you want an even more luscious result, add a tablespoon of butter after you've heated up the milk. You can use this custard to garnish fruit tarts and crostatas, stuff beignets, or make it into a cake filling. Or enjoy it as is with fresh fruit. It is also delicious mixed with an equal part of whipped cream or whipped coconut cream.

CLASSIC VANILLA CUSTARD

MAKES 3 CUPS (750 ML)

4 large egg yolks

⅓ cup (1.7 oz/50 g) potato starch

¾ cup plus 1 tablespoon (5.7 oz/ 160 g) packed light brown sugar

2 cups (500 ml) full-fat regular or almond milk

Peeled skin of ½ medium lemon

½ vanilla bean, seeds scraped

In a medium saucepan, place the yolks, potato starch, and brown sugar. Whisk well until the mixture becomes a smooth cream. In a separate small saucepan, place the milk, lemon peel, and vanilla bean pod and seeds. Warm the milk mixture over low heat until lukewarm—do not boil. Slowly whisk the milk mixture into the egg mixture, adding the vanilla bean and lemon peel as well, and heat over medium heat. Keep whisking the mixture slowly as the custard heats up, or it might stick to the bottom of the pan. As it starts to thicken, whisk more vigorously. When it thickens to the point that you feel some resistance when you are whisking, remove the pan from the heat. It will thicken more as it cools down. Cover the top of the custard with plastic wrap if you are not using it right away, and store it in the fridge.

FOR A LEMON VARIATION: Follow the recipe for the Classic Vanilla Custard but add the grated zest of 3 medium lemons and the juice of 2 lemons to the milk. For a stronger lemon taste, add the juice of the third lemon. You can also substitute water for the milk in this variation for an even lighter custard—it turns out wonderfully.

NOTE: I reduced the sugar from my family's original recipe, but should you want to go full swing, use a full cup (200 grams) of brown sugar. If you want a perfectly white custard, use white sugar, as other kinds of sugar will make it darker.

MAKING PASTA

If there is one memory most Italians have from when we were kids, it is the memory of hiding under the table while our mothers and nonnas made fresh pasta, whether it was gnocchi, strozzapreti, or fresh ricotta filling for ravioli. When I was small I could not wait to sneak out and eat a little piece of raw pasta and dash away again before my mother could see me and yell. My mother always said that eating uncooked pasta was "bad for digestion." As I grew older, I stopped hiding under the table and instead spent my Sundays with my hands in the flour, working with the women of my family, with the smell of sauce bubbling away.

Making your own pasta can be a bit labor intensive, but it is a great weekend activity and not that difficult if you own a pasta machine. Getting your pasta perfectly right will require some practice and maybe a little trial and error. But it's a deeply rewarding process, and, of course, homemade pasta is the best pasta!

CHOOSING THE RIGHT FLOUR FOR PASTA

Fresh pasta can technically be made with any flour. But to avoid soggy, mushy pasta, it is crucial to use good-quality flour. I like to use stone-milled when possible: Stone-milled flour has a less powdery, thicker consistency that gives the pasta the most wonderful texture. If the flour you are using is old, bleached, or too processed, the pasta might not turn out consistent and al dente. Read the label and make sure the flour is unbleached and does not contain any chemicals.

These days, I make my pasta with a mix that includes whole-wheat flour and often semolina flour. Using semolina flour will improve the final taste and texture, as its "mealy" consistency gives the pasta that rustic feel and will prevent it from breaking during cooking. (For more information on semolina flour and where to buy it, please see page 17.) If you cannot find semolina flour, use some good-quality, organic white or fine-milled whole-wheat flour, or experiment with the flour you have available. Try substituting one-quarter of the total weight of the flour with flours such as semolina, buckwheat flour, rye flour, chestnut flour, or chickpea flour.

You can make unique and delicious pastas by

Flour Mixes

SEMOLINA MIX

A good mix that works for all classic pastas.

—

1 part semolina flour (or good-quality white flour if you cannot find semolina, or a mix of both)

1 part whole-wheat flour

—

For 2½ cups (10.5 oz/300 g) of flour:

  1¼ cups (5.3 oz/150 g) semolina flour

  1¼ cups (5.3 oz/150 g) whole-wheat flour

OR:

  ⅔ cup (2.6 oz/75 g) semolina flour

  ⅔ cup (2.6 oz/75 g) white flour

  1¼ cups (5.3 oz/150 g) whole-wheat flour

100% WHOLE-FLOUR MIX

Flour mixes with added fiber and nutrition.

—

1 part whole-wheat flour

1 part other kind of non-gluten-free flour, such as spelt or rye flour

—

For 2½ cups (10.5 oz/300 g) of flour:

  1¼ cups (5.3 oz/150 g) whole-wheat flour

  1¼ cups (5.3 oz/150 g) whole-spelt or rye flour

MIXED FLOURS MIX

Flour mixes for those who want to get creative with flavors and alternative options.

—

1 part whole-wheat flour

1 part other kind of non-gluten-free flour, such as spelt or rye flour

1 part alternative flour, such as chestnut flour, chickpea flour, buckwheat flour, hemp flour, rice flour . . .

—

For 2½ cups (10.5 oz/300 g) of flour:

  ¾ cup + 1 tablespoon (3.5 oz/100 g) whole-wheat flour

  ¾ cup + 1 tablespoon (3.5 oz/100 g) whole spelt or rye flour

  ¾ cup + 1 tablespoon (3.5 oz/100 g) alternative flour

---

pairing together different flours. In the recipes in this book that call for handmade pasta, I will give you guidance on the best flours to use, but here are some of my favorite combinations.

NOTE: It is much better to use a scale rather than cups to measure out flour for pasta, as different flours (especially if stone-milled) usually have different volumes. If you only have cups available, you may have to do a little tweaking.

NOTE #2: If you can find it, use "00" or "0" Italian flour for making pasta. If not, good-quality, organic all-purpose flours will do.

MAKING THE DOUGH

What you will need:

- Your ingredients measured and ready
- A clean, spacious work surface
- Damp kitchen towels, to keep your dough from drying
- A long, flat knife, preferably with a rectangular blade, for cutting the pasta
- Cutting wheels and other tools for cutting pasta, depending on the kind of pasta you want to make
- Floured baking sheets for arranging your cut pasta

The basic rule for making dough is that every ¾ cup flour (3.5 ounces / 100 grams) will make enough pasta for one very hungry person or, in the case of stuffed pasta, enough pasta for two. A total of 2⅓ cups (10.5 ounces / 300 grams) flour will serve about four.

BASIC DOUGH

This dough is good for any kind of pasta. You can also add a flavor or coloring agent to this dough, such as a tablespoon or two of beet juice or tomato paste. *Serves 4*

——

Any of the flour mixes mentioned opposite
(2½ cups [10.5 oz/300 g] of flour total)

OR

2½ cups (10.5 oz/300 g) good-quality wheat flour

1 teaspoon olive oil

3 large eggs

Water, in case you need it

Pinch of salt

——

1. Place the flour on a wooden or marble work surface. Make a well in the center and add the olive oil and eggs. Whisk the oil and eggs with a fork or your fingers and start incorporating the flour a little at a time. You will end up with a ball of dough that falls apart, and at first it might seem like it is not wet enough. Knead well, pushing the dough against the work surface with the heel of your hand, collecting the bits and pieces of dough. Keep kneading vigorously, rotating the dough as you go, for at least 10 minutes. If after 5 minutes of kneading you cannot incorporate all of the flour, or the dough feels way too stiff, add water 1 teaspoon at a time, incorporating well after each addition. There will be some hardened bits of flour that you cannot

incorporate: Scrape those off the work surface and discard.

2. After 10 minutes, your dough should feel supple and smooth and damp in your hands. It is okay if it's not completely smooth—it will get smoother after it rests and after the second kneading.

3. Wrap the dough in plastic wrap, or put it in a ziplock bag or in an airtight container, and let it rest for at least 30 minutes on the counter, or up to overnight. If resting for over 30 minutes, transfer to the fridge. When you are ready to roll the dough, flour your board or work surface and vigorously knead the dough for 5 minutes.

EGGLESS DOUGH

This recipe is great to make with alternative flour mixes. Many regional pastas are made without eggs, and many contain a portion of chestnut flour, chickpea flour, or buckwheat flour, especially in the Italian Apennine and Alps. This creates a texture that works especially well for short or stuffed pasta shapes. *Serves 4*

——

Any of the flour mixes described above (works especially well with the Mixed Flours Mix, opposite)

Approximately ½ cup to ¾ cup (125 ml to 175 ml) water, as much as you need to make the dough come together

1 tablespoon olive oil

Pinch of salt

——

Put the flour and water in a large bowl and mix well, then vigorously knead the dough for 5 minutes, until the dough comes together. At this point, the dough might be quite dry. Add water 1 tablespoon at a time as you knead the dough: You should end up with a ball of dough that feels ever so slightly damp but is stiff and not sticky. Just like with eggless pasta, let it rest for at least 30 minutes, then knead it again before rolling it out, keeping the board or work surface well-floured.

ROLLING THE DOUGH

Divide the dough in half to make it easier to roll out with a pasta machine.

Prepare the setting: Clear some table or counter space and prepare some floured tea towels where you will lay out the prepared dough. Flatten out the dough with your hand, then pass it through the pasta machine on the largest setting.

Fold it in half, turn the knob to a thinner setting, and pass it through again. Dust the pasta with flour each time you pass it through. Repeat, turning the knob to a thinner setting, until you achieve the desired thickness. Lay the pasta sheet on the tea towel and proceed with the other half. Do not overlay the strips of pasta on the towels. If you are making stuffed pasta, wrap the second half of the dough in a damp towel and cut and stuff the pasta right away, before moving on to the second half.

HOW TO CUT TAGLIATELLE, TAGLIOLINI & PAPPARDELLE

Once you roll out the dough, let it rest for about 10 minutes to dry slightly.

Prepare a baking sheet with floured wax paper where you'll lay the finished pasta. Heavily flour all of the slightly dried dough strips and loosely roll the right and left edges toward the center, flouring the dough after every couple of rolls. Do not roll it tightly. When the two edges meet in the middle, it should look like a sort of rolled-up parchment. Generously flour the surface.

Time to cut the pasta: For best results, use a flat, long knife and hold it fast where the handle meets the blade. Slightly slide it on the board to cut even strands of pasta, cutting the "parchment" crosswise.

- FOR TAGLIOLINI: Cut twenty-five ⅛-inch-wide (3 mm) strips for one serving. Grab the cut pasta in the middle and gently shake it to unfold it. Make a nest and move it onto the baking sheet. Repeat until you run out of dough.

- FOR TAGLIATELLE: Cut twenty ¼-inch-wide (5 mm) strips for one serving.

- FOR PAPPARDELLE: Cut ½-inch-wide (1.5 cm) strips and count up to 13. Make each serving into a nest.

You can adapt these instructions for other cuts of pasta. For angel hair, cut the strips so they are half the size of tagliolini, or even finer if your dough is very pliable. Cut up to thirty for one serving. To make lasagnette, which are thicker than tagliatelle, cut eight 1-inch (2.5 cm) strips of pasta to make one serving.

HOW TO BOIL PASTA

To cook both fresh and dried pasta, you can follow the same cooking rules: Put 3 to 4 quarts of water im a large pot, cover, and bring to a rolling boil. Add the pasta and 1 scant teaspoon of salt for each quart of water you are using and gently stir. If the sauce you will be using is quite rich, add less salt.

For dry pasta, consult the package for cooking time. Fresh pasta usually takes no longer than 3 to 4 minutes, depending on its thickness. When the pasta floats to the surface, it is usually ready. Always test it a minute or two before it is

Buckwheat Pizzoccheri with
Chickpeas & Rosemary, page 77

Green "Strozzapreti"
with Cherry Tomatoes
& Aromatic Sauce,
page 155

supposed to be ready—you want to drain it al dente. If you cook it 30 seconds too long in the pot, the pasta will become soggy. Drained pasta should not be rinsed unless you want to make pasta salad. Have your sauce ready to toss the pasta in right away.

GENERAL PASTA-MAKING TIPS

- Keep the dough away from drafts and always keep it moist. The dough dries out very easily, and it's impossible to work with a dried-out dough.

- Knead your dough for at least a full 10 minutes. It's important not to skip this step.

- Always allow the dough to rest for at least an hour, either covered with a damp towel or sealed in a ziplock bag, to retain humidity. During resting time, the dough "relaxes" and the gluten has time to stretch out. If you are not using all of the dough in one go, or if you are making stuffed pasta, like ravioli, that requires precutting your dough, keep whatever dough you're not using covered with towels or with a plastic sheet.

- Always flour both the pasta and the work surface with white flour while you are working and cutting the dough.

- Add a pinch of salt or a teaspoon or two of olive oil into the pasta dough to improve flavor, though this is optional. If you have a rich sauce, definitely do not add the salt.

- If you are making stuffed pasta, always prepare the stuffing beforehand, even the day before.

Pasta-Making Troubleshooting Tips

Q: *My dough feels too dry or too soft. What should I do?*

A: If your flour-to-moisture ratio seems a bit off, all you have to do is a little tweaking. If it feels to dry, add a teaspoon or two of water. If it feels too soft, add an extra dusting or two of flour and knead the dough until it feels smooth and supple.

Q: *My pasta is ridged at the edges and tends to break.*

A: The dough is probably too dry to begin with, or it was left out uncovered for too long before the rolling or cutting step. Always keep a damp towel on hand to protect the dough, and keep it covered every moment you are not handling it.

Q: *My pasta sticks together!*

A: The dough is probably a little too wet. Dust it heavily with flour.

Q: *My pasta tends to break during cooking.*

A: This could happen for several reasons, but primarily it could be because the flour you used is either too old or low in quality. If you make pasta with cheap, bleached all-purpose flour, it is unlikely to stand up well to cooking. Another reason breakage can occur is if you use too much of a gluten-free flour. When there is too little gluten, the pasta does not stretch well and therefore tends to break.

FALL

Fall turns the countryside into a golden-hued, hazy dream. As the light of September dims, the colors go from bronze to orange and fade into a mist-shrouded pale glow when November settles in. We know that fall has knocked at our doors when we start seeing fat, dirt-specked porcini mushrooms at the market, when farmers from inland start displaying their first truffles, and when legume soups and tagliatelle find their way to town fairs.

Within the lush forest of Le Marche, which thrives with edible treasures, you can hear the sound of dogs pawing through the crisp leaves as they look for all kinds of mushrooms and, for the luckiest, chinks of white truffles. The thin veil of November fog shrouds the gold and red foliage, while the sun tries its best to shine through and hit the walls of our majestic old cities.

Back in the sixties, when my grandfather Ottavio was a kid, his family and he would brave the chill air on their Lambretta scooter to reach Urbino in Montefeltro, the Renaissance city where the famed painter Raphael was born and the place where his family had originated. They fit three people on the tiny scooter that was supposed to only host two: his dad in front, his mother on the backseat, while Ottavio sat sandwiched in between. The ride took over an hour, and they tried their best to hold their ragged coats closed against the November chill. The hills around the city, dark green with woods and dotted with tiny villages here and there, were the trading marketplace for not only all sorts of fungi but for local cheeses such as caciotta, ricotta stagionata, and pecorino di fossa, the biggest treasure of them all.

I imagine my grandpa, approaching the heavy doors that, when open, let out whiffs of damp wood and mold. He'd head into the *fosse*, or caves, lit by candles and lanterns. I imagine him moving the wood planks from the well in the center of the room and peeking in to see whole rounds of cheese wrapped in leaves and half-buried in hay. Fossa cheese is only produced in the Montefeltro area, and the special process to make it involves wrapping the cheese in cotton cloths and lowering it into ten-foot-deep wells in late August onto a stack of hay and aromatic herbs. There it is left to season for one hundred days.

But fossa cheese and truffles, which are still a strong tradition in the Montefeltro area, are merely two of the many things to celebrate the fall in Italy. In between Tuscany and Liguria, miles of chestnut forests grow lush and offer their fruits to make flour, which is traditionally used to make bread, pasta, and sweets. At the same time, families of farmers gather in the olive tree yards and cast their nets over the ground, then shake and rake the olive trees for the harvest. Fall is a chorus of people singing odes to the land, a dance that seems to celebrate new life in spite of the decay of the leaves and nature in the march toward winter. Life slows down, but it is one of the best times for cooking. In our kitchen, you'll find dishes pairing pumpkin and sage, rosemary and chickpeas, and pears and chocolate. We bake traditional sweets with the almonds, walnuts, and hazelnuts that were picked in September and are now dry enough to be added to breads and cakes. The air is filled with the scents of apples and *ciambelle*, making us look forward to Christmas.

The recipes in this chapter come from memories of my favorite season of the year. The smells of hearty casseroles coming from the windows, the sight of crispy leaves adorning monuments and castles, and baskets full of walnuts and hazelnuts. I think of taking strolls together along our stone-cobbled roads, wrapped in warm scarves, cones of hot roasted chestnuts warming our hands. I think of late Sunday mornings sipping cappuccino and evenings enjoying *vin brulé*, as October and November unfold before our eyes and we peacefully witness the days fading into winter.

RECIPES

Mains

Chickpea "Frittata" with Red Onions (V/GF)

Fall Tuscan Minestrone with Farro & Lots of Vegetables (V/GF)

Umbrian "Imbrecciata," a Thick Legume Stew (V/GF)

Pumpkin Orzotto, Vegetarian & Vegan Versions

Buckwheat Pizzoccheri with Chickpeas & Rosemary

"Boscaiola" Pasta Bake with Mushrooms, Peas & Truffle Oil (V)

Pumpkin Gnocchi with Sage & Pumpkin Seed Pesto (GF)

Sides & Salads

Black Rice & Buckwheat Salad with Nuts & Balsamic Herb Dressing (GF)

Roasted Root Vegetables with Nut Crumble (V/GF)

Fresh Porcini, Grilled or Sautéed (V/GF)

Broccoli "Strascinati" with Raisins & Nuts (V/GF)

Mushroom & Arugula Salad with Yogurt-Mustard Dressing & Cheese (GF)

Sweets & Desserts

Chocolate Cake with Pears (V/GF)

Buckwheat Cake with Berry or Fruit Jam (GF)

Chestnut & Chocolate "Fave dei Morti," the "Cookies of the Dead"

"Ciambellone Romagnolo," a Sweet Dipping Loaf

THIS WONDERFUL CHICKPEA FLOUR CONCOCTION, hailing from the past, is all the rage again in Italy right now. It is called *fari-frittata* (farina, "flour," plus the word *frittata*) because it resembles a regular frittata in color and consistency, but it is crispier and less fluffy—more like a thick pancake. Inspired by a traditional Ligurian dish called "Cecina" (or "Farinata" in other parts of Italy), which is cooked in very large round metal pans at country fairs with indulgent amounts of delicious olive oil, the rosemary in this recipe perfectly brings the chickpeas to the altar (but you can also change it up and use your favorite herbs instead). Add any thinly sliced vegetable you like along with or instead of the onion—just make sure you cook the veggies before adding them to the batter.

CHICKPEA "FRITTATA"
With Red Onions

....
SERVES 6
....

For the batter:

2 cups (6.5 oz/185 g) chickpea flour

3 tablespoons olive oil, plus more for the pan

½ teaspoon baking powder

1 teaspoon ground turmeric (optional)

1 tablespoon finely chopped fresh rosemary or parsley

1 teaspoon salt

Pinch of pepper

2½ cups (600 ml) water, preferably sparkling water

1 medium red onion, finely sliced

Add-ons:

Fresh Porcini Grilled or Sautéed (page 86)

Caramelized Onions (see Emilia-Style Vegetable Burgers, page 205)

Ligurian Pesto, Tomato Pesto, or Tapenade Dressing (page 43)

A drizzle of truffle oil

Finely chopped fresh parsley

1. **Make the batter:** Place the chickpea flour in a medium bowl with 1 tablespoon of the olive oil, the baking powder, turmeric (if using), rosemary, ½ teaspoon of the salt, and the pepper. Whisk the ingredients together. Slowly add the water while continuing to whisk, until the mixture turns into a smooth, thickish batter. Cover and let the batter rest in the fridge for at least 30 minutes. The batter can also be prepared the night before.

2. In the meantime, heat the remaining 2 tablespoons olive oil in a 9-inch (25 cm) nonstick pan over medium-low heat. Add the onion and sauté for about 10 minutes, stirring every 2 minutes, until the onion is translucent. Add the remaining ½ teaspoon salt, stir well, and cook the mixture for 10 to 15 minutes more, until golden. If the onions start to stick, add a small splash of water.

3. **When ready, cook the frittata:** You can cook it on the stovetop or in the oven. You need to use more oil when you bake it in the oven, but it gives the frittata a delicious crispy crust and an almost creamy interior. Both ways of cooking this chickpea delicacy are delicious.

recipe continues

4. To cook in a pan: Pour the batter into a 10-inch (26-cm) pan with the onions once they are ready. Cover and cook over medium-low heat for about 10 minutes, until the bottom is golden and set. Using a plate, flip the "frittata" and cook, uncovered, for 5 minutes more.

5. To cook in the oven: Preheat the oven to 475°F (245°C). Scrape the onion into the batter and mix well. Generously oil a 10-inch (25 cm) round baking dish or any baking dish that will let you spread the batter so that it's less than ½ inch (1.5 cm) thick. Bake for 15 to 20 minutes, until a crispy crust forms on top.

6. Slice the "frittata" and serve with the suggested toppings and a side salad.

EVERY TIME I MAKE MINESTRONE, I stop and think how amazing it is that such a humble dish became so popular outside of Italy. The main idea behind minestrone is the same as a quiche: It's a recipe designed to rid the fridge of all the vegetable scraps that have been sitting for too long and are starting to look sad and wilted. Feel free to throw whatever vegetables you have on hand into your minestrone—this version, enriched with herbs and Tuscan farro, makes for a wonderful fall soup.

FALL TUSCAN MINESTRONE
With Farro & Lots of Vegetables

SERVES 8

½ cup (3.5 oz/100 g) dried borlotti beans (or any other kind you like), soaked overnight, or 1 cup canned beans

3 tablespoons extra-virgin olive oil

1 garlic clove, crushed and peeled

1 small sprig of rosemary, fresh or dried, finely chopped

3 sage leaves, preferably fresh, finely chopped

2 bay leaves, fresh or dried

1 large onion, finely chopped

3 medium carrots, scrubbed and diced

1 celery stalk, diced

½ cup (3.5 oz/100 g) whole farro, soaked overnight

½ cup (125 ml) tomato sauce

½ celeriac bulb, peeled and cut into small cubes

1 large pumpkin wedge, cut into small cubes

1 bunch Swiss chard or Tuscan kale, finely chopped

1½ teaspoons coarse sea salt, or a scant tablespoon fine sea salt

1. If you are using fresh borlotti, place them to a pot with plenty of water, bring them to a boil over medium-high heat, and boil for about 30 minutes before adding them to the minestrone (see Note, page 15). If you are using canned beans, skip this step.

2. Heat the olive oil in a large pot over medium-high heat. Reduce the heat to low, add the garlic, rosemary, sage, and bay leaves, and cook for about 2 minutes; the mixture should smell very aromatic.

3. Add the onion, carrots, and celery and stir well. Sauté for 2 to 3 minutes, until the onion turns translucent.

4. If you are using fresh borlotti, add the precooked beans to the pot. If you are using canned beans, rinse them well and add them to the pot.

5. Drain the farro of its soaking liquid and add the farro to the pot. Stir for 1 minute, then add the tomato sauce and stir for 1 minute more. Add enough water to cover the ingredients, cover with a tight-fitting lid, and cook over medium-low heat for 15 minutes.

ingredients and recipe continue

Vegetable Stock (page 32) or water, enough to cover all ingredients by 2 inches

To serve:

Extra-virgin olive oil

Crusty bread slices, preferably whole-wheat or Pugliese

Grated Parmigiano, pecorino, or Grana cheese (optional)

6. Add the celeriac, pumpkin, Swiss chard, and enough stock to cover all of the ingredients by 2 inches (5 cm). Let the soup cook, half-covered, until the beans are cooked, about 1 hour. Add the salt at the end and adjust the seasoning to taste. Remove the bay leaf.

7. Serve in bowls and finish with extra-virgin olive oil and a piece of crusty bruschetta, or some cheese if using dairy. This minestrone soup tastes even better the next day!

VARIATION: You can use any other bean you like: cannellini, red beans, or black beans are great. You can also change the vegetables according to season: peas, green beans, or zucchini make especially good minestrone—just make sure they are vegetables with some bite. In the summer, try omitting the sage and use finely chopped basil instead, adding it either at the end of the cooking process or along with all the vegetables.

You can play around with the grains, too: Try small pasta or barley instead of the farro. Use brown rice for a gluten-free alternative.

THE NAME OF THIS SOUP, "Imbrecciata Eugubina'" evokes images of the wonderful region of Umbria, a land of green hills studded with medieval stone villages and castles. *Eugubina* means "from Gubbio," the town it originates from, while "Imbrecciata" is the gravel and brittle on the roads of the countryside through the fields, which is what this humble but hearty protein- and fiber-packed soup looks like. Enjoy it while you dream of sitting next to a crackling fire in a stone house under the cold, sunny Italian winter sky.

UMBRIAN "IMBRECCIATA"

A Thick Legume Stew

SERVES 6

½ cup (3.5 oz/100 g) whole farro or spelt

½ cup (3.5 oz/100 g) whole barley

½ cup (3.5 oz/100 g) fresh corn kernels

½ cup (3.5 oz/100 g) dried chickpeas

½ cup (3.5 oz/100 g) dried lentils

½ cup (3.5 oz/100 g) dried beans, any kind

½ cup (3.5 oz/100 g) split fava beans (or more beans)

¼ cup (60 ml) olive oil

1 large onion, finely chopped

2 medium carrots, finely chopped

1 celery stalk, finely chopped

1 cup (250 ml) tomato passata or canned tomatoes

1 large potato or sweet potato, diced

1½ teaspoons salt, plus more to taste

2 pinches of pepper, plus more to taste

1. In a large bowl, combine the farro, barley, and corn and add enough water to cover by 2 inches (5 cm). In another large bowl, do the same with the chickpeas, lentils, beans, and fava beans. Soak for at least 10 hours or up to overnight.

2. When ready to cook, discard the soaking water and rinse the grains and legumes thoroughly. Boil the grains and legumes over medium-high heat in two separate pots with water to cover until cooked, about 1 hour.

3. Meanwhile, heat the olive oil in a large pot over medium-high heat. Add the onion, carrots, and celery and sauté for about 5 minutes, until the onion is translucent. Add the tomato passata and sauté for 5 minutes more. Add the diced potato and 1 cup (250 ml) water and cook for 15 minutes. Add the grains and legumes, salt, pepper, and enough water to cover the ingredients by 1 inch (2.5 cm). Let the soup cook, half-covered, for 20 minutes more, until the consistency turns thick and almost creamy. Stir in the marjoram.

4. Add more water if the soup reduces too quickly, and adjust the salt and pepper to taste. You should end up with a thick, creamy stew.

Water or Vegetable Stock (page 32), enough to cover all the ingredients by 1 inch (10 to 15 cups [2.5 to 3.75 l])

A few sprigs of fresh marjoram, finely chopped

5. Traditionally, Imbrecciata is served with a thick slice of crusty bread, but I'm happy without the bread given how hearty this soup is. The perfect finish to this stew is a teaspoon of good extra-virgin olive oil per bowl.

VARIATIONS: You can substitute herbs such as rosemary, bay leaves, or sage for the marjoram. If you are using these herbs instead, add them when you sauté the onion, carrots, and celery.

If you cannot find all the grains and legumes, just use the same amounts of your favorite whole grains and beans, but make sure they all have similar cooking times. You can also make this grain- and gluten-free by using a plethora of different legumes.

ORZOTTO IS ONE OF THE FIRST DISHES I LEARNED ABOUT when I started cooking vegetarian. Barley, which is *orzo* in Italian, behaves very similarly to risotto, producing a lot of starch and a luxurious texture. But, unlike white rice, it has a very high fiber content and will not leave you with an after-meal slump. This orzotto is a perfect dish to have when pumpkin is in season and the weather just calls for a nice warm meal in a bowl to hold between your hands. Use whole barley instead of pearled for an even heartier (and healthier!) result (note that it will take about thirty minutes longer to cook).

PUMPKIN ORZOTTO
Vegetarian & Vegan Versions

SERVES 2

1 small onion, finely chopped

1 medium shallot, finely chopped

2 tablespoons olive oil

¾ cup (about 140 g) pearled (or hulled) barley

1½ cups (10.5 oz/300 g) delicata squash, cut into ½-inch cubes

½ teaspoon organic veggie stock powder or bouillon cube (if using water instead of stock)

½ teaspoon salt

Pepper to taste

2 cups (500 ml) Vegetable Stock (page 32) or water

1 cup (250 ml) unsweetened almond milk or regular milk

Chopped parsley and grated pecorino or Grana cheese (optional), to finish

1. In a 10-inch (25 cm) saucepan, cook the onion, shallot, and olive oil on medium-low heat for about 5 minutes, until the onion is translucent.

2. Add the barley and toss with a wooden spoon to toast it for 2 minutes. Add the squash, stock powder (skip if using vegetable stock), salt, and pepper and toss briefly before adding the stock. Reduce the heat to low and cook, covered, until all of the stock is absorbed. Add the almond milk, cover, and cook until the orzotto is creamy, stirring every 3 to 5 minutes. Pearled barley will be ready in 30 to 40 minutes, while hulled barley could take up to 1 hour. Check it often and, if the liquid dries out too quickly, add more stock or water. If there is too much liquid left, cook, uncovered, over low heat until all of the liquid evaporates. Adjust the salt, and stir in liberal amounts of parsley and grated cheese, if desired (use at least 2 tablespoons). Stir in some Balsamic Onions (page 231) for an added punch of flavor—they go especially well with this risotto if you finish it with cheese, as the savoriness contrasts the sweetness of the onions and pumpkin nicely. Serve with a simple green salad on the side.

CHICKPEAS AND ROSEMARY ARE A STAPLE COMBINATION in Italian fall cooking, and they make their appearance on most restaurant menus as soon as summer comes to an end. In this fresh pasta, the slight smoky flavor of the buckwheat perfectly complements the earthy flavor of the rosemary and chickpeas. It is a hearty dish for those Sundays when you stick your nose out and find the air is a little crisp, and just like that you see those first few brown leaves on the ground. Pizzoccheri is a kind of buckwheat pasta from Valtellina in northern Italy. Its short shape keeps it sturdy during rolling and cooking.

BUCKWHEAT PIZZOCCHERI
With Chickpeas & Rosemary

....

SERVES 3 TO 4

....

⅔ cup (5 oz/140 g) whole-wheat flour

⅓ cup (1.7 oz/50 g) white spelt flour

¼ cup (1 oz/30 g) buckwheat flour

½ teaspoon salt, plus more as needed

2 large eggs plus 1 large egg yolk

6 tablespoons (90 ml) olive oil

4 large garlic cloves, minced

2 sprigs of fresh rosemary, finely chopped (about 4 teaspoons chopped)

3 medium shallots, thinly sliced

Pinch of dried red pepper flakes (optional)

1½ cups (10.5 oz/300 g) cooked chickpeas

¼ cup (50 ml) white wine

½ cup (125 ml) Vegetable Stock (page 32), plus more as needed

Coarse salt, for the pasta water

1. Combine the whole-wheat flour, spelt flour, buckwheat flour, and a dash of salt on a work surface and make a well in the center. Add the eggs and the yolk in the center and whisk with a fork to incorporate the eggs with the flour. Knead well for about 5 minutes, until the dough is smooth. Wrap in plastic wrap and let the dough rest for at least 30 minutes, or in the fridge overnight.

2. Heat the olive oil in a large pan over medium-low heat and add the garlic and rosemary. Sauté to release their aroma for 1 minute, then add the shallots and sauté for 2 minutes more. Add the dried red pepper flakes (if using), the chickpeas, and the salt. Sauté for 1 minute and, once the chickpeas are well coated in oil, raise the heat to medium-high and deglaze with the wine. Once the wine has boiled down for a few seconds, add the stock, reduce the heat to medium-low, and simmer for about 15 minutes, until the stock has fully reduced and the sauce is quite creamy. If it evaporates too quickly, add more stock. If the sauce looks very liquid, simmer for a bit longer until it thickens. There should still be about 2 tablespoons of liquid left. Using a fork, mash about one-third of the chickpeas and stir well. Taste and adjust the salt if necessary.

recipe continues

3. Roll out the pasta dough according to the instructions on page 56. To make the pizzoccheri, you will have to make tagliatelle first. To make tagliatelle, follow the instructions on page 56. To make the pizzoccheri, unfold the cut tagliatelle and lay them flat on the cutting board. Then cut them into 1-inch-long strips. Spread them on a heavily floured baking sheet.

4. Bring a pot of water to a boil, and add salt in the proportion of 1 scant teaspoon for every 4 cups (1 l) water. When ready, cook the pizzoccheri for about 2 minutes and no more than 3 minutes, until they float to the surface. Transfer them from the pot to the sauce using a small colander. Sauté the pasta in the sauce over medium-high heat until the pizzoccheri are well combined with the sauce and heated through. Serve immediately, as they tend to dry out and clump a little if left to cool.

BAKED PASTA is a real Sunday classic in every Italian home In my household, baked pasta brings up memories of when I was little and my mom would bake a tray of South Italian–style rigatoni laden with ragù and mozzarella. I took this comforting casserole and transformed it with the flavors of Le Marche and its woodsy aromas of mushrooms and truffle, both so abundant during fall. *Boscaiola*, which roughly translates as "from the woods," is usually made with cream, but I substitute my fantastic vegan Béchamel Sauce (page 35).

"BOSCAIOLA" PASTA BAKE
With Mushrooms, Peas & Truffle Oil

SERVES 4 TO 6

For the sauce:

5 tablespoons (75 ml) extra-virgin olive oil

1 large garlic clove, peeled and crushed

1 large yellow onion, finely sliced

17.5 ounces (500 g) cremini mushrooms, or a mix of porcini, champignons, and button, half finely sliced and half coarsely chopped

1½ cups (7.7 oz/220 g) frozen peas

⅓ cup (80 ml) white wine

1½ teaspoons salt

¼ to ½ teaspoon pepper, or to taste

1 tablespoon truffle paste

For the pasta:

1 tablespoon coarse salt

10 ounces (200 g) large shell pasta, or any other short pasta you like

½ recipe Béchamel Sauce (page 35)

1 to 2 tablespoons fine bread crumbs

TIP: You can store the prepared sauce in jars and freeze it for later use.

1. Make the sauce: Heat the olive oil in a large pan. Add the garlic and onion and sauté over low heat for about 10 minutes. If they start to stick, add a splash of water or white wine. Stir in the mushrooms and peas. Raise the heat to medium and cook for 5 minutes. Deglaze the pan with the wine. Add the salt and pepper. Reduce the heat to low and cook for about 30 minutes, until the vegetables are soft and there is no liquid left in the pan. Discard the garlic, add the truffle paste, and mix well.

2. Prepare the pasta, assemble, and bake: Preheat the oven to 400°F (205°C). Bring a large pot of water to a boil. Add the salt and stir, then add the pasta and cook for 3 minutes less than indicated on the package. Drain the pasta and toss it into the pan with the sauce. Add half of the béchamel sauce and mix well.

3. Prepare a casserole dish that can tightly fit the shells and spread a layer of béchamel sauce on the bottom. Add the pasta, filling them with sauce, and top with the remaining béchamel sauce. Finish with the bread crumbs. Bake for 20 minutes, until golden on top. Enjoy straight out of the oven. This pasta tastes great the day after and freezes wonderfully.

TIP: For a spring variation, use asparagus instead of the mushrooms and leeks instead of onion. For a summer variation, substitute the mushrooms for zucchini or eggplant and add ½ cup (125 ml) Tomato Sauce (page 33) to the béchamel sauce. In the winter, try using broccoli instead of peas.

JUST LIKE ROSEMARY PAIRS WITH CHICKPEAS IN ITALIAN FALL COOKING, sage is the perfect partner for pumpkin and squash. Pumpkin gnocchi is a quintessential fall dish mostly known in the Emilia part of the Emilia-Romagna region, which is famous for the cultivation of several delicious kinds of squash. Delicata squash is used for this recipe: Its dense flesh makes for plump, al dente gnocchi, while its slight sweetness is perfectly complemented by the cheese. We make these gnocchi all the time with freshly harvested sweet squash from our garden.

PUMPKIN GNOCCHI
With Sage & Pumpkin Seed Pesto

SERVES 4

For the gnocchi:

1¾ lbs (800 g) delicata squash, peeled and cut into chunks

¾ cup (4.2 oz/120 g) whole-wheat flour, plus more as needed

1 large egg

1 cup (3.5 oz/100 g) pecorino, Grana, or Parmigiano cheese, grated

½ teaspoon salt

For the pesto:

½ teaspoon salt, or to taste

1 garlic clove

5 fresh sage leaves

1 tablespoon finely chopped fresh parsley

¼ cup (1.7 oz/50 g) toasted pumpkin seeds

½ cup (125 ml) extra-virgin olive oil

Coarse salt, for the gnocchi water

Grated pecorino cheese or other hard cheeses you like or extra-virgin olive oil, to finish

1. Make the gnocchi dough: Preheat the oven to 425°F (220°C). Place the squash on a rimmed baking sheet and bake for 15 to 25 minutes, until the squash is tender (cooking time will depend on the freshness of the squash). When ready, spread the squash chunks on a plate and let cool. Scrape the flesh from the skin and discard the skin.

2. Using a potato masher or a fork, mash the squash. Arrange it in a well on a work surface or in a bowl and add half the flour, the egg, the cheese, and the salt. Combine the ingredients and knead well, adding more flour as needed. The dough should be smooth and only very slightly on the sticky side. Depending on the squash you are using, you might need more flour. Wrap in plastic wrap and let it rest for 1 hour in the fridge.

3. Make the pesto: Combine the salt, garlic, sage leaves, parsley, pumpkin seeds, and olive oil in a small food processor and process until smooth. You can also make the pesto in a mortar and pestle: Pound the salt and garlic first, then add the sage and parsley and pound to a paste. Add the pumpkin seeds and olive oil and pound well until the pesto is as smooth as you like.

recipe continues

TIP: If you are not cooking the gnocchi right away, you can line them on a floured baking sheet and put them in the freezer, then transfer them to a freezer bag once they are fully frozen. You can boil them frozen—just allow 1 minute more of cooking time.

4. When the pesto is ready, generously flour a work surface. Take the gnocchi dough out of the fridge and divide it into three parts. Roll each part into a long log that is about ½ inch (1.5 cm) thick. Cut off ½-inch (1.5 cm) pieces and dust the pieces with flour as you cut them.

5. Bring a large pot of water to a boil and add coare salt in the proportion of 1 scant teaspoon for every 4 cups (1 l) water. Add the gnocchi in two batches. Stir them as they cook, as they tend to stick together. They are ready in about 3 minutes, once they float to the surface.

6. Drain, reserving the cooking water, and add the gnocchi to a bowl with the pesto and 3 tablespoons of the cooking water. Toss to coat evenly. If they seem too dry, add a splash more cooking water, until they form a cream with the pesto. Finish with extra-liberal amounts of grated cheese and/or extra-virgin olive oil.

THIS SIMPLE GLUTEN-FREE SALAD makes a perfect accompaniment for any simple meal, as well as cooked or fresh vegetables. It is perfect year-round, but I find the smoky flavor of buckwheat is a wonderful complement to the earthy flavors that are so characteristic of the fall season. Black rice, which is called *riso venere* in Italy, makes quite a stunning visual impact. I find this salad to be particularly pleasing with Roasted Root Vegetables with Nut Crumble (page 85).

BLACK RICE & BUCKWHEAT SALAD
With Nuts & Balsamic Herb Dressing

SERVES 4 TO 6 AS A SIDE; 2 TO 4 AS A MAIN

For the dressing:

¼ cup (60 ml) extra-virgin olive oil

3 tablespoons good-quality balsamic vinegar

1 tablespoon orange juice, or more to taste

⅓ cup (a large handful) packed fresh parsley, finely chopped

1 small sprig of fresh rosemary, finely chopped

1 or 2 garlic cloves, grated

1 heaping teaspoon honey mustard (optional)

Salt

For the roasted nuts:

½ cup (2.8 oz/80 g) hazelnuts, coarsely chopped

¼ cup (1.4 oz/40 g) pine nuts

8 to 10 walnuts, coarsely chopped

1 tablespoon fresh or dried rosemary, finely chopped

1 teaspoon dried red pepper flakes, if you like some spiciness (optional)

1 tablespoon olive oil

2 pinches of salt

Pepper

⅔ cup (5 oz/140 g) cooked black rice

½ cup (3.5 oz/100 g) cooked buckwheat

Salt

1. Make the dressing: Combine the olive oil, vinegar, orange juice, parsley, rosemary, garlic, honey mustard (if using), and salt to taste in a jar and shake well. Set aside to let the herbs and garlic release their flavor.

2. Roast the nuts: Preheat the oven to 400°F (205°C). Toss the hazelnuts, pine nuts, walnuts, rosemary, red pepper flakes (if using), olive oil, salt, and pepper to taste on a rimmed baking sheet to coat evenly. Bake for about 8 minutes,

until brown. Keep a close eye on them, as they can go from done to burnt in a second.

3. To assemble: Toss the black rice, buckwheat, and salt to taste in a large serving bowl together with the nuts and the dressing. Serve with Roasted Root Vegetables with Nut Crumble (page 85), add Balsamic Onions (page 231), serve as is as a side, or add your favorite cooked vegetables to make it a delicious and hearty one-bowl meal.

THIS HAS ALWAYS BEEN my mom's go-to way to make potatoes: tossed with olive oil and bread crumbs, which gives them an unusually crunchy but satisfying finish. I added some nuts to make the texture even better, and replaced the potatoes with mixed root vegetables, but feel free to use potatoes of any kind for this classic Sunday side. For a gluten-free option, use coarse polenta meal instead of the bread crumbs.

ROASTED ROOT VEGETABLES
With Nut Crumble

SERVES 6 TO 8 AS A SIDE

4 pounds (about 2 kg) mixed root vegetables, such as turnips, beets, carrots, sweet potatoes, or celeriac, cubed

½ cup (125 ml) Crumb Topping "Alla Romagnola" (page 49)

½ cup (80 g) mixed nuts (pecans, walnuts, almonds, hazelnuts . . .), very finely chopped

¼ cup (50 ml) olive oil

1 teaspoon salt

½ teaspoon pepper

2 sprigs of fresh rosemary, finely chopped

1 sprig of fresh thyme or marjoram, very finely chopped (optional)

1. Steam or boil the root vegetables for 8 to 10 minutes, until they start to get tender. In the meantime, preheat the oven to 400°F (205°C).

2. Toss the root vegetables on a rimmed baking sheet with the crumb mixture, mixed nuts, olive oil, salt, pepper, rosemary, and thyme (if using). Bake for 25 to 30 minutes, until nicely roasted and crispy on the outside.

NOTE: I prefer to keep the skins of the vegetables on, but if they are very dirty or have crevices that you cannot clean well, remove those or peel the vegetables altogether.

AS MID-OCTOBER KICKS IN, the markets start displaying basketfuls of these precious mushrooms, brought by passionate mushroom hunters from the hills of Urbino, Acqualagna, and all the inland villages of Le Marche. The best way to cook porcini, aside from using them to make a good bowl of tagliatelle, is to just grill them with olive oil or quickly sauté them in a pan.

When choosing porcini, make sure that they are firm, smell fresh, and have no yellow sponge on the gills. Scrub them clean with a soft brush and remove with a knife any dirt that sticks. Clean them thoroughly with a damp towel, then thinly slice them lengthwise.

FRESH PORCINI
Grilled or Sautéed

SERVES 4 AS A SIDE,
OR ENOUGH TO MAKE PASTA SAUCE FOR 2 OR 3 AS A MAIN

Dressing:

¼ cup (60 ml) extra-virgin olive oil

2 garlic cloves, finely sliced

¼ cup (a small bunch) packed fresh parsley (2 tablespoons finely minced)

½ teaspoon salt

Pepper to taste

17.5 ounces (500 g) fresh porcini mushrooms

To finish:

A splash of apple cider vinegar or to taste

A drizzle of Savory Balsamic Glaze (page 50)

1. Make the dressing: Combine the olive oil, garlic, parsley, salt, and pepper to taste in a jar and shake well. Prepare it at least an hour in advance (or the day before) so that the garlic and parsley can flavor the oil.

2. Make the mushrooms: Heat a grill or nonstick pan and cook the mushrooms until soft, about 2 minute per side. Transfer to a plate.

3. To finish: Add the vinegar to the dressing, shake well, and drizzle the mushrooms with liberal amounts of the dressing. Finish with a drizzle of Balsamic Glaze. The mushrooms make a wonderful side with Polenta al Tagliere Three Ways (page 112) and on Chickpea "Frittata" with Red Onions (page 64).

4. For a mushroom pasta sauce variation: Thinly slice an onion and sauté it in a large pan over medium heat with the olive oil, garlic, parsley, salt, and pepper for about 10 minutes, until soft. Coarsely chop the mushrooms instead of slicing them, and sauté them with the onion. Add ½ cup (125 ml) water and cook, half-covered, for 20 minutes more. Uncover, stir well, and let all of the water fully evaporate. Boil your favorite pasta and toss it in the pan with the mushroom sauce to coat evenly. If you wish, finish with some grated Grana and a teaspoon of truffle paste before serving.

NOTE: Don't have porcini mushrooms? Follow the same recipe using sliced portobello mushrooms or any other sliceable mushroom you like or have available.

WHEN I LIVED IN NEW YORK, I had a flatmate who told me a story about how shocked she was when, during a trip to Italy, she saw her host mother cooking the life out of broccoli.

"I had never seen anything like it before!" she said. "She cooked it until almost mushy, with tons of garlic. It was delicious!"

And it is. Strange as it may sound, and although it is surely not the healthiest way to cook broccoli, do give this a try. You will be amazed at how even broccoli can become what tastes like an indulgent, olive oil–laden, garlicky treat.

BROCCOLI "STRASCINATI"
With Raisins & Nuts

SERVES 4 AS A SIDE

Florets from 2 large heads broccoli, or about 2 pounds (900 g)

¼ cup (60 ml) olive oil

3 large garlic cloves, crushed

1 small onion, finely sliced

1 tablespoon packed light brown sugar

3 tablespoons balsamic vinegar

1 teaspoon salt

¼ teaspoon pepper

⅓ cup (1.7 oz/50 g) raisins, soaked and squeezed out

¼ cup (50 ml) water

⅓ cup (1.7 oz/50 g) pine nuts or almonds, toasted

1. Blanch the broccoli florets in boiling water for 5 minutes or, even better, steam them for 10 minutes.

2. Heat the olive oil in a large pan over medium-low heat and add the garlic. Sauté for about 2 minutes, until the garlic releases its aroma. Add the onion and sauté for 5 minutes, until translucent. Add the broccoli and stir to coat with the oil, then add the brown sugar, vinegar, salt, pepper, and raisins. Stir well to dissolve the sugar, add the water, reduce the heat to low, and let cook, half-covered, for 30 minutes. If the broccoli dries out too much, add a splash more water. Uncover and cook for 5 minutes more, until any leftover water has evaporated and the broccoli is very soft and slightly caramelized. Sprinkle the toasted nuts on top.

VARIATION: For an extra-simple version of this dish, omit the vinegar, raisins, and pine nuts. It will be just as delicious.

I LOVE PREPARING THIS QUICK SALAD when local mushroom hunters make their appearance at the market with their baskets full of champignons. This versatile side has appeared on many of our holiday tables as a fuss-free dish to ease the fatigue of preparing a big meal, but it can also be part of an everyday lunch or supper along with some simply cooked beans, lentils, or grains. The arugula gives it a nice peppery kick, while the tang of the yogurt-mustard dressing has always reminded me of the north of Europe. And with good reason: My mom prepared this often for German tourists who stayed at the hotel she worked at, who joyfully ate every last bite. The recipe calls for just a tiny bit of yogurt, which is mellowed down by the olive oil. Feel free to add more yogurt if you prefer a tangier dressing.

MUSHROOM & ARUGULA SALAD
With Yogurt-Mustard Dressing & Cheese

SERVES 6 AS A SIDE

For the dressing:

¼ cup (50 ml) plain yogurt

1 heaping teaspoon Dijon mustard

5 tablespoons (75 ml) extra-virgin olive oil

1 teaspoon salt

Juice of ½ lemon

2 sprigs of fresh thyme or marjoram

1 garlic clove, very finely minced (optional)

For the salad:

1 pound (450 g) mushrooms, such as champignons or button mushrooms

3 cups (about 3.5 oz/100 g) packed arugula

Shaved Grana cheese, to top

1. Make the dressing: In a small bowl, combine the yogurt, mustard, olive oil, salt, lemon juice, thyme, and garlic (if using), and whisk well. It keeps, refrigerated, for a few days, should you want to make a bigger batch.

2. Make the salad: Scrub the mushrooms clean with a vegetable brush and a damp, soft tea towel. Peel the outer skin if the mushrooms are a bit tough and not too fresh. Otherwise, make sure you clean them thoroughly. Slice them quite thinly—it is easier to do this with a mandoline slicer.

3. Toss the mushrooms with the arugula, top with liberal amounts of shaved Grana, and add dollops of dressing.

4. Serve with any fall or winter main dish, or toss with some cooked beans and farro or brown rice for a one-bowl meal. Pecorino cheese or crumbled blue or goat cheese are also great.

FOR A VEGAN VARIATION: Use unsweetened plant yogurt instead of regular yogurt, or cashew cream if you want a more luscious dressing. Omit the cheese and top with lightly toasted walnuts instead.

WE HAVE TWO SMALL PEAR TREES IN OUR ORCHARD, and, as with most fruit trees, we never know how much fruit they will yield each year. A couple of years ago, they produced no pears at all. Last year, one of them produced only three pears, but I swear they were the best pears I have ever tasted in my life. This year, their branches were bent with a blessing of lots of crispy, sweet pears. I used many of them to make this decadent cake. Pear and chocolate is my favorite flavor combo, and it is always a hit with everyone who tries it.

CHOCOLATE CAKE
With Pears

MAKES ONE 9-INCH (22-CM) CAKE

For the pears:

5 small Williams (Bartlett) pears

1 tablespoon packed dark brown sugar

2 tablespoons lemon juice

1 tablespoon rum (optional but strongly recommended)

¼ teaspoon ground cinnamon, or more to taste

For the batter:

⅓ cup (75 ml) organic flavorless sunflower oil or melted coconut oil, plus more for greasing the pan

4 large eggs, separated

1 cup (7 oz/200 g) packed dark brown sugar

1 cup (4.5 oz/130 g) whole spelt (or wheat) flour

¼ cup (1 oz/30 g) unprocessed cocoa powder

¼ cup (1.5 oz/40 g) potato starch

2 teaspoons baking soda

½ cup (125 ml) plain yogurt, regular or plant

2 teaspoons vanilla extract

2 ounces (60 g) dark chocolate, melted

1. **Prepare the pears:** Peel, core, and cut the pears into small cubes, saving some thin slices to decorate the top of the cake later. In a large pan, combine the pear cubes with the brown sugar, lemon juice, rum (if using), and cinnamon. Cook over medium-high heat, tossing frequently, for about 5 minutes, until the juices evaporate and the pears are tender. Set aside to cool.

2. **Make the batter:** Preheat the oven to 350°F (180°C). Grease a 9-inch (22-cm) springform pan with sunflower oil.

3. Add the yolks in a large bowl with ½ cup (100 g) of the brown sugar. Beat with a stand or handheld mixer for about 5 minutes, until the yolks are pale and frothy and have doubled in size. In a separate large bowl, combine the flour, cocoa powder, potato starch, and baking soda and sift the mixture into the eggs, folding until incorporated. In a medium bowl, combine the yogurt, sunflower oil, and vanilla. Fold the yogurt mixture into the batter. Add the melted chocolate and the remaining ½ cup brown sugar and fold the batter into the cooked fruit.

4. In a large bowl, beat the egg whites until stiff with a stand or handheld mixer and gently fold them into the batter by making a slow upward circle motion until fully incorporated.

5. Pour the batter into the pan. Tap the pan on a table to remove air bubbles, and scatter the pear slices you saved on top. Bake for about 45 minutes, until a toothpick inserted in the center of the cake comes out clean.

THIS IS A CAKE FOR THOSE WHO LIKE ROBUST, SMOKY FLAVORS with real character. Hailing from the alpine regions of Italy, where buckwheat is largely used, this gluten-free treat is light enough to serve as a special breakfast with a cup of black tea. The original version calls for red currant jam and heavy cream, but I added an apple to the dough to make the cake moister and chose a tart berry jam for the filling (though any other berry jam works well). The smell as it bakes in the oven makes me think of wooden huts nestled in the mountains, cinnamon cookies, and cozy fireplaces.

BUCKWHEAT CAKE
With Berry or Fruit Jam

MAKES ONE 10-INCH (25-CM) LOAF

½ cup (125 ml) vegetable or coconut oil, plus more for greasing the pan

⅓ cup (2.1 oz/60 g) buckwheat flour

½ cup (3.2 oz/90 g) brown rice flour

⅓ cup (1.7 oz/50 g) whole-wheat or rye flour (or substitute more rice flour for gluten-free)

⅓ cup (1.7 oz/50 g) almond flour

1 cup (7 oz/200 g) packed dark brown sugar, plus more to sprinkle on top

2 teaspoons (10 g) baking soda

1 heaping teaspoon ground cinnamon

Grated zest of 1 lemon

4 large eggs

1 medium apple, grated

½ cup (125 ml) almond milk, hazelnut milk, or soy milk

1 teaspoon vanilla extract

¾ cup (175 ml) raspberry, tart cherry, cranberry, or other fruit jam of your choice

Almond slivers, to decorate

1. Preheat the oven to 350°F (180°C). Line a 10-inch (25-cm) loaf pan with parchment paper and lightly grease it with vegetable oil.

2. In a large bowl, combine the buckwheat flour, brown rice flour, whole-wheat flour (if using), almond flour, ½ cup (100 g) of the brown sugar, the baking soda, cinnamon, and lemon zest and whisk to combine.

3. Crack the eggs into another bowl and add the remaining ½ cup (100 g) brown sugar. Using a handheld or stand mixer, beat for at least 5 minutes, until the mixture is pale and has doubled in size.

4. Add the flour mixture to the eggs a little at a time, stirring gently with a spatula. The dough will get very dense. At this point, add the grated apple, vegetable oil, almond milk, and vanilla and fold in.

5. Pour in the batter into the prepared loaf pan and distribute it evenly with the spatula. Dollop tablespoonfuls of the jam along the batter, and marble the cake by dipping the tablespoon a few times into the batter. Sprinkle with brown sugar and slivered

recipe continues

sheet at least 1½ inches (4 cm) apart and push them down gently with two fingers to make them a little flatter. You will need to bake them in batches.

6. Cook for 20 to 25 minutes, or until flattened and golden on top. They will be very soft straight out of the oven, so check the color to make sure they are ready. Let cool before enjoying.

FOR A CLASSIC VARIATION: To make the classic version (as in the photo), just substitute white flour for the chestnut flour and leave out the cocoa powder and chocolate chips. Add the grated zest of 1 small lemon to the dough.

FOR AN ORANGE VARIATION: Follow the directions to make either chocolate or classic *Fave dei morti*. Add the grated zest of 1 medium orange and ⅓ cup (1.7 oz/50 g) finely chopped candied orange peel to the dough.

CIAMBELLONE, A RUSTIC LOAF-SHAPED CAKE that is quite dense, is the most traditional sweet in Romagna. It is probably one of the first things you learn to bake if you have a *nonna* from Romagna. Flavorwise, it is kind of reminiscent of a vanilla coffee cake, and it always makes an appearance at any birthday, festivity, or country fair. Its texture makes it perfect for dipping—at local festivals, you'll always find elderly people dipping slices of it in glasses of sweet wine. The most traditional version was made with lard, but many other recipes started to make their way into the kitchens of the region: Some people make it with vegetable oil, others with olive oil. Some varieties have chocolate chips and cocoa, and so on. Because it is already a rather dense loaf, I like to mix in a hefty, unprocessed flour like spelt or oat flour to make the ciambellone even more flavorful. If you want to stick to a really traditional version, use stone-milled local all-purpose flour.

No matter what recipe you decide to use, make sure you have a glass of sweet wine, coffee, or milk at hand!

"CIAMBELLONE ROMAGNOLO"
A Sweet Dipping Loaf

SERVES UP TO 20 PEOPLE

1½ cups (8.8 oz/250 g) whole-wheat flour

1½ cups (8.8 oz/250 g) spelt or rye flour

4 large eggs, 1 separated

1 cup (190 g) brown muscovado sugar, plus more for sprinkling on top

½ cup (125 ml) mixed oil (two-thirds vegetable oil and one-third olive oil)

2 teaspoons baking soda

1 teaspoon baking powder

2 teaspoons vanilla extract

Grated zest of 1 lemon

Almond milk or regular milk, enough for the dough to come together

1 cup (6.2 oz/165 g) dark chocolate chips (optional)

Chocolate variation:

¼ cup (3.5 oz/30 g) cocoa powder

½ cup (2 oz/60 g) dark chocolate chips

1. Preheat the oven to 350°F (180°C). Line a baking sheet with parchment paper.

2. Combine the whole-wheat flour, spelt flour, the 3 whole eggs and 1 egg white, sugar, vegetable oil–olive oil blend, baking soda, baking powder, vanilla, and lemon zest in a food processor and process until the dough comes together. You can do the same in a large bowl and knead with your hands. You should end up with a dough that holds together but is a little sticky. If the dough is too tough or not sticky, add a splash of milk. Fold in the chocolate chips (if using), and knead briefly to distribute them evenly. If the dough is the right consistency, it will stick a lot to your hands and make a bit of a mess.

3. Scrape the dough onto the prepared baking sheet. Add 1 tablespoon water to the leftover egg yolk and whisk briskly with a fork. Dip a wet brush in the yolk and, with a combination of the brush and your wet hands, shape the dough into an oval loaf. Sprinkle sugar on top and bake for about 40 minutes, until golden. Check with a toothpick to make sure it comes out clean and the ciambellone is cooked through. Wait for it to cool before slicing.

FOR A CHOCOLATE VARIATION: Reserve half the dough and knead it again with the cocoa powder and dark chocolate chips, then scrape the cocoa dough on top of the regular dough. This way, the chocolate part always comes out slightly denser than the white part, but this is how every grandma did it!

WINTER

The countryside in the winter is covered in a thick blanket of fog and frost. A remote quietness permeates the air, and every step and whisper echoes among the fields. After dancing and singing the beauties of fall, December's cold drives us home to nest in front of a burning fireplace, doors shut closed against the chill.

Excitement builds as we wait for the upcoming festivities to start. Christmas is just around the corner, and all the towns dress up with lights and begin to fill with markets, sellers of hot chocolate, and crepe stands. My favorite winter afternoons are spent strolling along the alleys of the castle of Gradara, which is decorated like a castle in a fairy tale with all sorts of lights, roses, and ribbons. Brightly lit pastry shops decorate their windows with all sorts of traditional cookies and cakes, like the heavily spiced panforte and panpepato, cookies like Tuscan cantucci; then torrone (nougat), dried fruit, almond paste–covered cakes, and chocolate pralines. The scent of mulled wine is everywhere, emanating from large barrels stationed outside wineshops and trattorias. From now until a couple of weeks after New Year's, we will warm our hands around glasses of hot wine and eat slices upon slices of pillowy panettone or pandoro.

The farming world has few rituals in the winter. It is time for the ground to rest—the deepest sleep before the awakening of spring. Though the vegetable garden might look dead in late winter, it brims with radicchio, bitter greens, brassicas, and tubers—all vegetables that, as my grandfather would always say, "need to get frosty to be good." We make up the shortage of fruit with the beautiful citrus shipping up from southern Italy. We cook dishes loaded with greens and enjoy winter vegetable pizza by the fire. By the time February rolls around, winter's long nights make us desperate for the revelry and excitement of Carnevale in February and March.

But first, winter celebrations bring dishes that are a little more fanciful to our table. Starting with the Feast Day of the Immaculate Conception on December 8 and ending with New Year's Day, this festive season is filled with traditional recipes accumulated over the years, passed down from Italian grandmothers to each new generation. Baking and roasting dominate, and desserts and sweets to celebrate the season are abundant.

These are the recipes that are deeply linked to our Italian winters: cookies and baked goods, hearty lunches, and dinners with friends and family, followed by a warming espresso and a pour of sambuca. They remind me of gazing out the window after a special holiday meal, waiting for a much-expected snowflake to fall, as the table, lined with decorated tablecloths that are only pulled out once or twice a year, host people playing cards among bread crumbs and clementine peels, the smells from the oven and scents of oranges still in the air.

RECIPES

Mains

Creamy Sunchoke Soup with Golden Onions (V/GF)

Zuppa del Nord, an Earthy Baked Cabbage Soup

Pasta with Herb Butter Sauce & Toasted Pine Nuts

Polenta al Tagliere Three Ways: Beans, Mushroom Sauce, Truffle Oil (V/GF)

Risotto with Radicchio & Walnuts (V/GF)

Blue Cheese Pizza with Radicchio & Balsamic Glaze

Cabbage Parcels with Lentils & Onions (V/GF)

Sides & Salads

Chicory "Al Coccio" with Tomato Sauce & Olives (GF)

Fennel Gratin with Saffron & Nuts (V)

Winter Salad with Fennel, Blood Oranges & Nuts (V/GF)

Warm Brassica Salad with Tapenade Dressing (V/GF)

Caramelized Brussels Sprouts & Lentil Salad, Sweet & Sour (V/GF)

Sweets & Desserts

Chocolate Mousse, Scented with Orange (V)

Apple Roll with Jam & Walnuts

Tiramisu: Pistachio & White Chocolate

Classic Biscotti, Tuscan "Cantucci"

IF YOU ARE UNFAMILIAR WITH THIS WINTER ROOT, it is totally worth a try: Similar to ginger in shape, its taste is reminiscent of artichoke (hence its alternative name, Jerusalem artichoke), but it has a texture similar to potatoes, which makes it perfect for creamy soups or purees. Sunchokes contain lots of fiber and are especially high in inulin, a kind of fiber that makes you feel full for longer. They also contain a good amount of minerals (especially potassium) and vitamins, so this soup is perfect for a simple, nourishing everyday meal.

CREAMY SUNCHOKE SOUP
With Golden Onions

SERVES 4 AS AN APPETIZER OR 2 AS A MAIN

For the onions:

1½ tablespoons olive oil

2 medium onions, finely sliced

1 tablespoon apple cider vinegar or white wine vinegar

1 teaspoon packed light brown sugar

½ teaspoon salt

Pepper

For the soup:

1 pound (450 g) sunchokes

1 small potato

1 tablespoon olive oil

1 small sprig of fresh rosemary, or 1 teaspoon dried rosemary

2 sage leaves, fresh or dried, finely minced

2 medium shallots, finely sliced

3 cups (750 ml) Vegetable Stock (page 32)

1 scant teaspoon salt

Pepper

1 cup (250 ml) almond milk

Chopped pistachios, for garnish

Shaved Parmesan cheese, for garnish

1. Make the onions: Heat the olive oil in a medium pan over medium-low heat. Add the onions and sauté for 5 minutes. Add the vinegar, brown sugar, and 2 tablespoons water. Reduce the heat to low and cook, stirring often, for about 30 minutes, until the onions turn a rich gold color. Add the salt and pepper to taste toward the end and stir well.

2. Make the soup: Thoroughly wash the sunchokes and potato under running water and scrub them clean with a brush. (I prefer to use them with the skin on, but make sure they are thoroughly clean.) Cut the sunchokes and potato into chunks, keeping the cut pieces submerged in water while you prepare the rest.

3. Heat the olive oil in a large pot over medium-high heat, then add the rosemary and sage and sauté for 2 minutes, until aromatic. Add the shallots and cook for about 5 minutes, until the shallots become translucent. Add the sunchokes and potato, stir them in the pot, then add the stock, salt, and pepper to taste. Cook over medium heat for 25 to 30 minutes, until the vegetables are very tender.

4. Remove the pot from the heat. Add the almond milk and blend until smooth using a blender or an immersion blender.

5. Serve in bowls and top with the onions. Serve with a slice of toasted sourdough bread or with some lentils. Or add any grain of your choice and a legume to make it a complete meal.

VARIATION: If you want a lighter soup, replace the potato and one piece of sunchoke with a sliced leek and skip the olive oil: instead of sautéing the vegetables, just add all of the ingredients for the soup to the pot and let them simmer until soft.

THIS SOUP IS INSPIRED BY THE THICK WINTER FLAVORS OF THE ALPS, where cabbage, potatoes, and melty cheese are widely used ingredients. In the Alps, cows are free to graze in vast green fields and so the quality of dairy is top-notch. There are many kinds of wonderful cheeses crafted with love. For this baked soup, fontina is the perfect cheese. If you cannot find it, use any good quality melty cheese that you love (Taleggio, Brie, Gorgonzola, and any blue cheese are some wonderful options). You do not need much of it—the gently browned onions provide a kick of flavor that makes the cabbage shine.

ZUPPA DEL NORD
An Earthy Baked Cabbage Soup

SERVES 4

4 medium yellow onions, finely sliced

6 tablespoons (90 ml) olive oil

½ cup (125 ml) white wine

1 medium head of cabbage, weighing about 1 pound (450 g), finely sliced into 1 x 1-inch pieces (2.5 cm x 2.5 cm)

2 medium potatoes, weighing about 10.5 ounces (300 g), cubed

8 cups (2 l) Vegetable Stock (page 32)

2 teaspoons salt, or more or less to taste

4 heaping tablespoons (about 3.5 oz/30 g) grated Grana cheese

4 thick slices whole-rye or buckwheat bread

One or two ⅛-inch (3 mm) slices Fontina cheese per bowl

1. Place the onions and the olive oil in a medium pot and sauté over medium-low heat, stirring often, for about 10 minutes, until the onions are golden. The onions will release some moisture first, then start to stick to the bottom. When they do, deglaze the pot with ¼ cup (50 ml) of the wine and stir well. Cook for 10 minutes more to cook off the wine, then deglaze with the remaining ¼ cup wine. Cook for about 10 minutes more, until the onions are nicely browned but not caramelized.

2. Add the sliced cabbage to the pot and toss with the onions. Sauté for about 5 minutes, until the cabbage is wilted.

3. Reduce the heat to low, add the stock and salt, cover, and cook, stirring every now and then, for about 50 minutes, until the mixture has thickened. Add the grated cheese and mix well.

4. Preheat the broiler and prepare four single-serving deep ovenproof bowls. Add a slice of bread to the bottom of each bowl, cover with the soup, and finish with a thin slice of fontina. Broil the soup for about 3 minutes, until the cheese melts and slightly blisters on top. Serve immediately.

FOR A PIZZOCCHERI SOUP VARIATION: Skip the rye bread and broiling step and add 2 cups (7 oz/200 g) Buckwheat Pizzoccheri with Chickpeas & Rosemary (page 77) about 5 minutes before the soup is done cooking.

ONE THING THERE IS NEVER A SHORTAGE OF here in the countryside are wild herbs and aromatics, which grow both in my garden and all around the fields all year long. When the coldest months of winter strike and the vegetable garden needs some rest, the comforting aroma exuding from their freshly snapped stalks spreads and fills the kitchen and reminds us that nature is far from dead. I love to awake the dormant spirit of spring with dishes like this pasta—so quick to make that the longest task will be boiling the water—and inhale the aroma wafting from the pan, as if I were breathing in the scents from our rosemary and sage bushes.

PASTA WITH HERB BUTTER SAUCE
& Toasted Pine Nuts

SERVES 2

¼ cup (1.2 oz/35 g) pine nuts

Coarse salt, for the pasta water

3½ tablespoons (50 g) butter

3 tablespoons olive oil

1 tablespoon minced fresh rosemary

1 tablespoon minced fresh sage

1 teaspoon minced fresh thyme

1 teaspoon minced fresh marjoram

Grated zest of ½ organic lemon

12 ounces (320 g) fresh pasta (tagliolini, angel hair, or tagliatelle)

½ teaspoon fine sea salt

Pepper

¼ cup (1 oz/30 g) grated Pecorino cheese

1. Heat a small pan over medium-high heat. When the pan is hot, place the pine nuts in the pan and dry-toast them by tossing them, shaking them often, for about 2 minutes. When they start to render their oil and turn slightly brown, they are ready. Set aside.

2. In the meantime, bring a large pot of water to a boil and add coarse salt (a scant teaspoon every 4 cups [1 l] water).

3. Melt the butter with the olive oil in a medium pan over medium-low heat and add the rosemary, sage, thyme, marjoram, and lemon zest. Let the butter foam slightly and the herbs release their aroma, about 2 minutes. When the herbs have sizzled slightly, remove the pan from the heat.

4. Boil the pasta in the salted water according to the package instructions (or until it floats to the surface, if it is fresh pasta).

5. Place the pan with the herbs and butter over medium heat. Drain the pasta, reserving the pasta water. Add the pasta to the pan. Add about ¼ cup (50 ml) pasta water and stir the pasta to form a creamy base with the fat and starchy water. Adjust the salt if needed.

6. Finish with freshly cracked black pepper and the cheese. Serve immediately and garnish each dish with the toasted pine nuts and more lemon zest, if desired.

POLENTA, A WELL-LOVED TRADITIONAL DISH throughout Italy, is especially big in Veneto. My great-grandmother, who was from Chioggia, used to cook it the old way: in a large copper vat in the fireplace, stirred with a long wooden paddle. After an hour of cooking, my grandmother would pour the polenta onto a large wooden tray, and when it was set she would cut it with sewing thread. Nowadays, these cooking methods are a little difficult to replicate, but if you have a large wooden cutting board, you can serve this polenta on it with all of the assorted toppings. It makes a wonderful presentation for a dinner party.

POLENTA AL TAGLIERE, THREE WAYS

Beans, Mushroom Sauce, Truffle Oil

SERVES 4 TO 6

For the polenta:

8 cups (2 l) water

1 tablespoon salt

17.5 ounces (500 g) polenta (preferably whole-meal if you can find it)

For the stewed beans:

17.5 ounces (500 g) borlotti beans, soaked overnight

1 small onion, cut in half

1 celery stalk, cut into three pieces

1 large carrot, cut into three pieces

1 small potato

1 cup (250 ml) tomato passata

4 cups (1 l) Vegetable Stock (page 32)

4 cups (1 l) water

1½ teaspoons salt

2 teaspoons pepper

1. Make the polenta: Heat the water in a tall pot until it steams and starts to simmer. Add the salt, dissolve it, and wait for the water to start slightly simmering again. Add the polenta to the water a little at a time and, as you add it, whisk vigorously with a whisk or wooden spoon. For the first 5 minutes, keep stirring the polenta. After that, give the polenta vigorous stir every 5 minutes or so. The polenta will take about 40 minutes to cook completely. You will know it is ready when it is thick and smooth.

2. Immediately pour the polenta into three deep dishes and wait for it to cool. Or, for a fancier alternative, pour the polenta onto a large wood cutting board and spread it evenly with a spoon.

FOR THE STEWED BEANS VARIATION: Drain the beans and add the beans to a large pot. Fill the pot with water to cover by 1 inch (2.5 cm). Bring the water to a boil over medium-high and let boil for 2 minutes, then drain and discard the water. Return the beans to the pot (or to a clay pot if you have one) and add the onion, celery, carrot, potato, tomato passata, stock, and water. Let cook over low heat, half-covered, until the beans are very soft, about 1½ hours, giving the beans a stir every now

For the mushroom sauce:

2 whole medium porcini mushrooms, fresh or frozen (or substitute dried—see recipe)

2 garlic cloves, finely minced

2 heaping tablespoons finely chopped fresh parsley

¼ cup (60 ml) olive oil

17.5 ounces (500 g) mixed mushrooms, cleaned and coarsely chopped

⅓ cup (75 ml) white wine

1 teaspoon salt

½ teaspoon pepper

¼ cup (50 ml) heavy cream, plus 1 tablespoon butter for finishing (optional, but nice)

For the grilled polenta:

Liberal amounts of truffle olive oil, flaked sea salt, and freshly ground black pepper, or 1 heaping teaspoon truffle paste dissolved in ¼ cup (50 ml) extra-virgin olive oil

NOTE: These stewed beans are not only a perfect topping for polenta, but they are also great with boiled pasta and rice, or add some stock and make soup. You can freeze these beans by dividing them into glass jars and thawing them whenever you need some.

and then. After 1 hour of cooking, add the salt and pepper and mix well.

Once ready, scoop out the onion, carrot, celery, and potato with a slotted spoon and transfer them to a blender. Add one-third of the cooked beans to the blender as well. Blend to a smooth puree and return the mixture to the pot. Serve over the polenta.

FOR THE MUSHROOM SAUCE VARIATION: Slice the porcini mushrooms ¼ inch (5 mm) thick and chop into ½-inch (1.5 cm) pieces. (If you cannot find fresh porcini, use about ¼ cup (about 5 g, or a small handful) dried porcini, soak for 1 hour in warm water, and finely chop, reserving the soaking water.)

Place the garlic, parsley, and olive oil in a medium pan over medium-high heat and sauté for about 1 minute, until aromatic. Add the porcini and other mushrooms, stir for 1 minute more, and add the white wine. Let the mixture fully reduce over medium heat, then add the salt, pepper, and ¼ cup (50 ml) of the soaking water. Reduce the heat to medium-low, cover, and cook for 10 minutes, then uncover and stir. Add another ¼ cup (50 ml) water, cover, and cook for 10 minutes more. Add a little more water if the mushrooms stick to the pan. When ready, uncover and stir the mushrooms until any liquid left is fully evaporated and the mushrooms brown slightly. Serve the mushroom sauce over the polenta.

FOR A GRILLED POLENTA VARIATION: Heat up a grill until hot (or use a cast-iron skillet). Once the polenta is set, cut it in ½-inch-thick (1.5 cm), 2-inch-long (5 cm) slices and very lightly oil them. Grill them for about 5 minutes per side, until crispy and slightly brown. Serve drizzled with truffle oil.

Grilled polenta can also be used instead of bread to make bruschetta. Top it with any topping you would use for that purpose, including Caramelized Onions (see Emilia-Style Vegetable Burgers on page 205) or any pesto in the basic recipe section (Ligurian Pesto, Tomato Pesto, or Tapenade, page 43).

THIS HEARTY WINTER DISH has its roots in the region of Veneto, known for its radicchio and its rice plantations. Risotto always reminds me of my Venetian origins and of my great-grandmother, who worked as a *mondina*, a girl in charge of hand-harvesting rice in the rice fields. She would bring back bags of Vialone Nano rice, which made the creamiest, richest risotto. I sometimes make this with brown risotto rice, but, while this variation is delicious and satisfying, I am not sure how happy my great-grandmother would be to see her traditional risotto made this way. If you prefer to stick to my great-grandmother's recipe, use the best-quality risotto rice you can find—either Vialone Nano or Carnaroli.

RISOTTO
With Radicchio & Walnuts

SERVES 2

3 tablespoons olive oil

½ medium onion, finely minced

1 small shallot, finely sliced (optional)

¾ cup (5.3 oz/150 g) brown or white risotto rice (Vialone Nano or Carnaroli)

1 medium head radicchio

2 to 3 cups (500 to 750 ml) Vegetable Stock (page 32)

½ teaspoon salt, or more to taste

⅓ to ½ cup (1.7 oz/50 g to 2.1 oz/ 60 g) aged meltable cheese, such as Asiago, Taleggio, or blue cheese (use 1 tablespoon nutritional yeast if vegan)

4 to 6 walnuts, some finely chopped and some coarsely chopped

1. Heat the olive oil in a medium pot over medium heat and add the onion and shallot. Sauté for 5 minutes, then add the rice. Stir for 2 minutes to let the rice toast, then add the radicchio and stir for 2 minutes more. Add 1 cup (250 ml) of the stock and the salt and stir. Reduce the heat to medium-low and cook the risotto, half-covered, for about 10 minutes, until the first cup of stock is well absorbed. Add an additional ½ cup (125 ml) of stock and wait for about 5 minutes more for it to be fully absorbed. Stir delicately, and repeat the process until the rice is fully cooked. It should take 35 to 50 minutes total, depending on the quality of the rice.

2. When the rice is done and the liquid has been fully absorbed, add the cheese and let it melt. Add 2 to 3 of the walnuts and stir to combine. Taste for salt and add some to taste if the cheese is not savory enough.

3. Serve in individual plates and top with the remaining walnuts. It is delicious the day after and freezes very well, too.

THIS IS REAL COMFORT FOOD for a winter weekend night when you feel like pizza and want to try your hand at making some. The slight bitterness of radicchio and the tangy savoriness of blue cheese are wonderfully complemented by the sweetness of the balsamic glaze. I dare anyone to classify this beautiful pizza pie as junk food! It is a classy Italian twist on a standard pie with sophisticated flavors. If blue cheese is too much for you, consider using smoked Scamorza instead.

BLUE CHEESE PIZZA
With Radicchio & Balsamic Glaze

MAKES 2 LARGE PIES

1 recipe dough from Quick Pizza (page 46)

For the vegetables:

2 tablespoons olive oil

1 garlic clove, crushed

1 medium onion

1 medium head of radicchio (preferably of the Chioggia variety; see Note), finely sliced

½ teaspoon salt

For the pizza toppings:

½ cup (2.1 oz/60 g) crumbled blue cheese, such as Gorgonzola, or more to taste

Sweet Balsamic Glaze (see Sweet & Savory Balsamic Reductions & Glaze on page 50), for drizzling

1. Prepare the pizza dough according to the basic recipe.

2. **Prepare the vegetables:** Place the olive oil and garlic in a medium/large pan and sauté over medium heat for about 1 minute, or until aromatic. Add the onion, reduce the heat to medium-low, and sauté for 10 minutes. Add the radicchio, stir, and cover. Let the mixture cook for about 5 minutes, or until the radicchio is wilted. Add the salt, stir well to coat evenly, and cook for 5 minutes more.

3. Once the pizza dough is arranged on the baking sheets, top each pie with the vegetables. Bake one at a time for 20 minutes, then take out the pie and top with the blue cheese. Bake for 5 to 8 minutes more, until the cheese is bubbling and melted. Slice the pizza, drizzle with a little balsamic glaze, and serve.

NOTE: Choose radicchio of the Chioggia variety, as Trevigiano could be a little too bitter for some.

WHEN I WAS FRESH OUT OF SCHOOL, I spent a year working as a personal assistant in the home of a Hungarian woman who had been a cook her entire life and had been lead chef for many Italian restaurants and hotels. But her favorite recipes hailed from her home country. I remember once she cooked traditional stuffed rolls called *toltott kaposzta*, which involve a generous amount of smoked pork. Stuffed cabbage leaves are a common dish in many countries (northern Italy included). Her recipe is the inspiration for this delicious vegetarian version I created—no pork in my take. The lentils give this dish earthiness while the spices give it richness, and the soft, juicy texture easily surrenders to the teeth and warms your heart and stomach.

CABBAGE PARCELS
With Lentils & Onions

MAKES 6 PARCELS

For the parcels:

6 large cabbage leaves

2 tablespoons olive oil

1 small onion, finely chopped

1 garlic clove, finely minced

½ medium carrot, finely chopped

3 tablespoons tomato paste

1 teaspoon finely chopped fresh parsley or basil

½ teaspoon dried marjoram

¼ teaspoon ground coriander

1 teaspoon ground turmeric

1 teaspoon sweet paprika

½ teaspoon salt

¼ teaspoon pepper

1 cup (7 oz/200 g) cooked lentils

1 cup (7 oz/200 g) cooked brown rice

3 heaping tablespoons Grana or pecorino cheese

2 tablespoons whole-wheat bread crumbs

6 chives, to tie the parcels (optional)

1. Make the parcels: Fill a large pot with water and bring to a boil over medium-high heat. Briefly blanch the cabbage leaves in the boiling water for 3 minutes. Drain, rinse, and set aside.

2. Heat the olive oil in a medium pan over medium heat and add the onion. Sauté until translucent, about 5 minutes, then add the garlic and carrot. Sauté for 5 minutes, then add the tomato paste and stir to dissolve. Reduce the heat to medium-low and cook, covered, for 5 to 8 minutes more, until the tomato paste is caramelized and all of the vegetables are soft. Stir every few minutes to make sure the mixture does not stick.

3. Add the parsley, marjoram, coriander, turmeric, paprika, salt, and pepper and stir well. Remove the pan from the heat and add in the lentils, rice, cheese, and bread crumbs. Stir well to mix. It should form a somewhat sticky filling.

4. Lay the cabbage leaves out flat on a clean surface and spoon an even amount of the filling into the center of each leaf. Fold the left and right edge of each cabbage leaf so that the two sides just cover the filling, then fold over each bottom and roll them up to form a parcel. You can leave them untied or tie each with chives, if desired.

ingredients and recipe continue

BAKED FENNEL HAS BEEN A STAPLE on our overcrowded holiday table ever since I can remember, scattered amid roasts, sautéed greens, and bread baskets on our table. We had a metal tray dedicated to baking it, and I remember the heaps of fennel piled and loaded with oil, béchamel sauce, and cheese. I always found it a little on the heavy side for my digestion, so I never ate much. As our home cooking evolved, though, we learned to appreciate fennel's licorice-y flavor and stopped pairing it with heavy sauces and cheese. While the version with béchamel sauce is indeed delicious (the recipe for Spring Pasticcio with Leeks & Cipollini on page 171 is very similar), this delicious saffron dish lets the fennel flavor really shine. When I first tried it, I knew I had found my new favorite recipe for the holidays.

FENNEL GRATIN
With Saffron & Nuts

SERVES 6 TO 8 AS A SIDE

4 medium fennel bulbs (about 2½ pounds (1.2 kg) total weight)

Pinch (1 g) of ground saffron

¼ cup (60 ml) olive oil, plus more for drizzling

1½ teaspoons salt

2 pinches of pepper

2 pinches of ground nutmeg

⅓ cup (75 ml) Crumb Topping "Alla Romagnola" (page 49; use polenta meal if gluten-free, adding 1 extra tablespoon olive oil)

1 teaspoon dried marjoram or thyme

⅓ cup (1.4 oz/40 g) pistachio nuts or almonds, ground

NOTE: If you want to give this dish some extra flair, sprinkle ⅓ cup (1.2 oz/30 g) grated Grana or Parmesan on the fennel before baking.

1. Trim the hard tops off the fennel bulbs and remove any brown skins. Wash them thoroughly and cut them in half, then cut each half into three wedges. Steam or boil the fennel for 10 minutes, until fork-tender but still firm. Drain and let cool for 10 minutes, then place in an 8 × 12-inch (20 × 30-cm) casserole, or any casserole dish that can fit the fennel slices in a single layer.

2. Preheat the oven to 400°F (205°C).

3. In a small bowl, dissolve the saffron in the olive oil and add the salt, pepper, and nutmeg. Toss the fennel slices with the saffron oil and the bread crumbs in the casserole dish, and then spread them so that they overlap as little as possible. Sprinkle evenly with the marjoram. Top the fennel slices with the ground nuts and drizzle with a bit more olive oil. Bake for 15 to 20 minutes, until the top is golden and the edges are slightly caramelized. You can broil the fennel for about 2 minutes for extra crunch.

FOR A VARIATION WITH BÉCHAMEL SAUCE: Skip the nuts and crumb topping, and toss the fennel in the casserole with 1 cup (250 ml) Béchamel Sauce (page 35). Sprinkle on ⅓ cup (1 oz/30 g) grated Grana and bake according to the above recipe.

THIS SIMPLE BUT BRIGHT AND FLAVORFUL SALAD is the perfect base for a light meal, or it can be a delicious side to a rich dish. Orange and fennel salad is a quintessential dish in wintertime in Italy, and its fragrant anise-y aroma from the fennel, which contrasts so well with the sweetness of the oranges, evokes images of all the citrus gardens that are heavy with fruit in our coastal towns, which are never cold enough for snow. The salad is then blessed by golden drops of fruity olive oil, which adds roundness to all the flavors. The walnuts are also essential to this salad and give it a wonderful, hearty crunch. Here I decided to use blood oranges: I love their ruby, jewel-like red in contrast to the white of the fennel—call it Snow White salad if you like. This salad is also perfect for a healthy *merenda*—the Italian afternoon snack.

WINTER SALAD
With Fennel, Blood Oranges & Nuts

SERVES 4 TO 6 AS A SIDE

For the dressing:

6 tablespoons (90 ml) fruity extra-virgin olive oil

2 tablespoons orange juice or lemon juice

1 teaspoon apple cider vinegar

¼ teaspoon salt

Pinch of pepper, or to taste

For the salad:

2 medium blood oranges

3 medium fennel bulbs, finely shaved

8 to 10 walnuts, or ½ cup (1.2 oz/60 g) mixed nuts, toasted

¾ cup (2.1 oz/75 g) pecorino or Grana cheese shavings (optional)

½ cup (125 ml) Marinated Olives (page 232; optional)

Salt and pepper

1. **Make the dressing:** Combine the olive oil, orange juice, vinegar, salt, and pepper in a jar and shake well.

2. **Prepare the vegetables:** Peel the oranges with a paring knife in order to get rid of the white parts as well. Cut them lengthwise into ¼-inch (5 mm) slices. Or, if you prefer, cut them crosswise to show the sections of the orange, which look beautiful in the salad. Toss the shaved fennel and sliced oranges in a bowl with the walnuts, pecorino (if using) and olives (if using). (I find that marinated olives and pecorino shavings really take this salad up a few notches: Their salty kick complements the sweetness of the orange wonderfully.) Add the dressing and toss well. Adjust the salt and pepper to your liking. (The amount of salt you'll want to add to this salad largely depends on whether you add olives and pecorino, which are quite salty themselves.)

NOTE: I like to julienne the fennel using a mandoline to get really fine shavings.

THIS IS A WONDERFUL AND WARM WINTRY SALAD that is a perfect side to any fall or winter main dish, when broccoli, cauliflower, and my absolute favorite, romanesco peek out of their massive leaves from the plants in our vegetable garden. The garlicky tapenade dressing brings the memories of summer flavors to this cold-weather salad.

I also like to add some lentils or other pulses or grains sometimes to make this salad a one-bowl meal. Add your favorite chopped, toasted nuts or seeds for extra crunch.

WARM BRASSICA SALAD
With Tapenade Dressing

SERVES 4 TO 6 AS A SIDE

12 ounces (340 g) broccoli florets (a small head)

12 ounces (340 g) romanesco florets (a small head)

12 ounces (340 g) cauliflower florets (a small head)

1 heaping teaspoon salt

Lemon juice

For the dressing:

3 tablespoons extra-virgin olive oil

1 garlic clove, finely sliced

4 or 5 pieces of tomatoes preserved in olive oil, very finely chopped

2 tablespoons Tapenade Dressing (page 43)

Salt

1. Wash the broccoli, romanesco, and cauliflower florets well. Bring a large pot of water to a boil over high heat and add the salt. Add the florets and cook for about 15 minutes, until tender. (You can also steam them instead of boiling. Just skip the salt and add more to taste later.)

2. **Make the dressing:** In a small pan over low heat, place the olive oil and garlic. Lightly sauté the garlic for about 2 minutes to release its aroma. (If you have a good tolerance for garlic, mince the garlic instead of slicing and sauté for just 1 minute.) Add the chopped tomatoes, stir for 1 minute, and add the tapenade. Remove the pan from the heat and stir well to mix. Add salt according to your taste and how salty your tapenade is.

3. Drain the florets and let them sit for 10 minutes to fully dry. Toss in a bowl or serving dish with the dressing and a squeeze of lemon juice. Serve warm.

NOTE: You can make this a full meal by adding 1 cup of cooked grains or pulses (I love this with whole-wheat couscous) and toasted nuts or seeds to your liking.

I LEARNED TO APPRECIATE BRUSSELS SPROUTS in the United States, and when I returned home I immediately introduced them to the other cruciferous vegetables we grow in our garden. I love Brussels sprouts with lentils and shallots in this recipe. They really shine in this sweet-and-sour, delicious one-bowl meal. Rich and hearty, it is one of those recipes that usually wins over the hearts of even die-hard meat eaters. You can also pair the lentils with broccoli, cauliflower, or romanesco instead of Brussels sprouts.

CARAMELIZED BRUSSELS SPROUTS & LENTIL SALAD
Sweet & Sour

SERVES 4 AS AN APPETIZER, 2 AS A MAIN

1½ cups (10.5 oz/300 g) brown lentils

1½ pounds (700 g) Brussels sprouts

10 large shallots

3 tablespoons olive oil

2 tablespoons balsamic vinegar

1 tablespoon honey or maple syrup

1 teaspoon salt, plus more as needed

½ teaspoon pepper

Almond slivers, for garnish

Savory Balsamic Glaze (page 50) to top

Drizzle of extra-virgin olive oil, for finishing

2 sprigs of fresh thyme or marjoram (optional)

1. Place the lentils in a large pot and cover them with water by at least 1 inch (2.5 cm). Bring the water to a boil over medium-high heat. Reduce the heat to medium-low and simmer until the lentils are tender but still retain their shape. The time varies depending on how fresh the lentils are. It could take 20 to 30 minutes, so taste them to check around the 20-minute mark. When they are ready, drain them, briefly run them under cold water, and set aside in a fine-mesh strainer to dry.

2. Preheat the oven to 400°F (205°C).

3. Wash the Brussels sprouts and trim off any damaged leaves. Trim at the root end and make a shallow cross incision on the bottom of each one. Steam them for 10 minutes, or until they start to get tender on the outside.

4. Peel the shallots and cut them in half, cut off the tough root, and cut each half in half again. Toss on a rimmed baking sheet with the Brussels sprouts, olive oil, vinegar, honey, salt, and pepper and mix well with your hands to coat evenly. Roast for about 30 minutes, until tender and slightly caramelized.

5. When ready, toss everything together in a large bowl with the lentils. Finish with a handful of toasted almond slivers, a drizzle of balsamic glaze, and thyme if you wish. Adjust the salt if necessary, and add one more drizzle of extra-virgin olive oil.

A SIMPLE, OLD-FASHIONED, intensely chocolaty dessert that has all the flavors and smells of winter-time, this is the kind of recipe you would find in vintage Italian cookbooks or in a *nonna*'s notebook. With the chocolate and orange pairing, this version is a fresh twist on the classic. It's an extremely adaptable mousse, easy and quick to make, so use your imagination to come up with other flavor combinations you'll love.

CHOCOLATE MOUSSE
Scented with Orange

SERVES 4

⅓ cup (1.7 oz/50 g) white, wheat, or spelt flour

⅓ cup (1.4 oz/40 g) unsweetened cocoa powder

4 to 5 tablespoons (1.4 to 1.7 oz/ 40 to 50 g) packed dark brown sugar

Grated zest of 1 medium orange

Pinch of salt

½ cup (125 ml) warm almond milk

3 tablespoons Grand Marnier or rum (substitute orange juice if you do not want to use alcohol)

7 ounces (200 g) dark chocolate (70 to 85% cocoa solids), broken into small pieces, plus more, shaved, to garnish

½ cup (125 ml) coconut cream (see Note) or heavy cream

2 tablespoons powdered sugar

⅓ cup (75 ml) candied orange peel, finely chopped, plus more to garnish

1. Sift the flour and cocoa powder into a medium pot and add the brown sugar, orange zest, and salt. Little by little, while whisking constantly, add the almond milk, then the Grand Marnier, until you have a smooth, thick cream. Try to avoid lumps.

2. Over low heat, bring the mixture to a simmer, stirring constantly. Add the dark chocolate and simmer while whisking vigorously for 5 minutes, or until very thick. If you see that the custard is sticking to the bottom the pot, remove the pot from the heat. It might look like lumps are forming, but keep whisking and the custard will eventually thicken into a smooth cream. If you stop for just a few seconds, the custard will stick.

3. Remove the pot from the heat and keep whisking for 1 minute more. Set aside to cool.

4. In a separate bowl, beat the coconut or regular cream with the powdered sugar until stiff and fluffy (see Note). When the custard has completely cooled, add 2 tablespoons of the cream to the custard and mix to loosen it up, then gently fold in the rest of the cream. Refrigerate for at least 1 hour before serving.

5. Garnish with candied orange peel and shaved chocolate.

NOTE: To make coconut cream: Refrigerate a can of coconut milk overnight, so that the fatty part can rise to the surface. Carefully scoop it out into a bowl with a spoon, avoiding any of the liquid. Whip the coconut fat as you would regular cream.

FOR A COFFEE VARIATION: Omit the liqueur or orange juice and the orange zest. Add 3 tablespoons espresso, or dissolve 1 heaping teaspoon coffee powder in the almond milk before adding.

FOR A MINT VARIATION: Skip the liqueur and orange zest and add 2 tablespoons chopped mint or to taste. Garnish with shaved white chocolate.

THIS RECIPE COMES OUT OF THE NOTES I found in my grandma's jam-and-honey-stained note-books when I was rummaging through them for inspiration. It is probably the most indulgent sweet recipe in my repertoire along with the Tiramisu: Pistachio & White Chocolate (page 137) and one my mother demanded I did not change or "healthify." We make this dense, rolled-up version of an apple pie only once a year, usually a month after harvesting walnuts from our trees, or around Christmastime. The feeling of biting into a slice of this—the juicy apple and soft crumb in your mouth while jam drips down your chin—is second to none. It is a perfect dessert for a winter party and will fill your home with the fragrant smell of apples, cinnamon, and toasted nuts.

APPLE ROLL
With Jam & Walnuts

MAKES ONE 11-INCH (28-CM) RING CAKE

For the cooked apples:

3 large red apples, peeled, cored, and finely sliced

1 tablespoon packed dark brown sugar

Juice of ½ lemon

1 teaspoon ground cinnamon

For the dough:

1¾ cups (8.8 oz/250 g) whole spelt (or wheat) flour

2 cups (8.8 oz/250 g) white spelt (or wheat) flour, plus extra for dusting the work surface and dough

4 large eggs

1 cup (7 oz/200 g) packed dark brown sugar, plus extra for topping

2 teaspoons baking powder

1 teaspoon baking soda

½ cup (4 oz/110 g) butter

1. Prepare the apples: Place the apples in a large pan and add the brown sugar, lemon juice, and cinnamon. Cook over medium heat for about 10 minutes, until the fruit softens. Set aside to cool.

2. Make the dough: In a food processor or in a large bowl, combine the spelt flours, eggs, brown sugar, baking powder, baking soda, butter, ⅓ cup (75 ml) Marsala, lemon zest, and vanilla until the dough comes together. The dough should be quite sticky but manageable. It will look a little looser than it should, but the softer it is, the better it will turn out once it is baked.

3. Preheat the oven to 350°F (176°C). Grease and flour a 11-inch (28-cm) round baking pan or Bundt pan.

4. Place a sheet of wax paper on your work surface, dust it with flour, and scrape the dough onto it. Dust the dough with more flour and top it with one more sheet of wax paper. Roll out the dough into a rectangle shape, sandwiched in between the two sheets of wax paper.

ingredients and recipe continue

⅓ to ½ cup (75 ml to 125 ml)
Marsala or white wine (use milk if
you do not want to use alcohol),
enough for the dough to come
together

Grated zest of 1 lemon

2 teaspoons vanilla extract

For the filling:

Cooked apples (from first part
of recipe)

1 cup (250 ml) peach, apricot,
or fig jam

1 cup (4.2 oz/120 g) shelled walnuts,
half finely chopped and half
coarsely chopped

5. To assemble: Remove the top wax paper sheet. Spread the jam and the apples on the dough evenly, leaving a 1-inch (2.5 cm) space along the borders. Sprinkle the walnuts evenly on top and roll the cake as delicately as possible into a log shape. Pinch the ends closed. To set the dough in the pan, arrange the log in a spiral, in a snail sort of shape. Place the baking pan on top and flip the dough gently into the pan. Brush the top with a little water, sprinkle with some extra brown sugar, and bake for about 40 minutes, until the cake has puffed up and is golden brown on top. Let the cake cool completely (this is very important!) before taking the roll out of the pan. Make thick slices for easier serving.

6. I love it by itself as it is quite rich, but add a dollop of yogurt or ice cream on top for a truly heavenly treat.

TIRAMISU IS *THE* ITALIAN DESSERT. It is thick and voluptuous, heavy yet fluffy, and delicious beyond description—I just had to include it in this book. We make tiramisu only once or twice a year for the holidays, and that is enough to have us dreaming of it for the rest of the time. This version is made with no eggs and a delicious mix of pistachio and white chocolate. Serve this wondrous treat for an important occasion or for the holidays.

TIRAMISU
Pistachio & White Chocolate

SERVES 8; MAKES ONE 8 × 8-INCH (20 × 20-CM PAN, 2 INCHES (5 CM) IN HEIGHT, OR 8 INDIVIDUAL CUPS

For the mascarpone cream:

5 ounces (140 g) good-quality white chocolate

1 cup (8.8 oz/250 g) fresh mascarpone cheese

2 to 3 tablespoons powdered sugar

½ cup (125 ml) pistachio butter (see Note)

1 cup (250 ml) heavy cream

1 teaspoon vanilla extract (optional)

To assemble:

20 Savoiardi cookies (see Note, page 138)

6 espresso shots diluted in ½ cup (125 ml) water, or ½ cup (125 ml) freshly brewed strong coffee

2 tablespoons packed light brown sugar

2 ounces (55 g) white chocolate, thinly shaved

½ cup (2.1 oz/60 g) whole pistachios, very finely chopped

1. **Make the mascarpone cream:** Melt the white chocolate in a glass or metal bowl over a pot of boiling water, making sure the bowl does not touch the water (or use a double boiler). In another bowl, add the mascarpone. Slowly pour in the melted chocolate. Add 1 tablespoon of the powdered sugar and the pistachio butter and mix well with a balloon whisk to incorporate.

2. In a separate bowl, whip the heavy cream with another tablespoon of the powdered sugar until stiff, then delicately fold it into the mascarpone mixture. Taste and check for sweetness: depending on how sweet your white chocolate is, you might want to add the third tablespoon of powdered sugar.

3. **To assemble:** Have the Savoiardi cookies and mascarpone cream close at hand. Pour the coffee into a shallow bowl—you will need to dip the entire length of the cookies in the coffee. Very quickly dip each cookie on both sides in the coffee, and line them on the bottom of an 8 × 8-inch (20 × 20 cm) serving dish. Do not soak each side for longer than a second, as the Savoiardi absorb a lot of liquid and might make your tiramisu too moist. You can break them up to make them fit the shape of the container you are using.

recipe continues

NOTE: Savoiardi are pillowy, thick, crispy cookies made mostly out of egg whites and sugar. They can usually be found at specialty Italian food stores or large supermarkets. Should you not be able to find them, you can substitute any kind of sponge cake, cut into slightly less than ½-inch-thick (1.5 cm) slices.

You can also make the tiramisu in individual pretty glasses, each holding about 1 cup (250 ml) in capacity. You should obtain 8 servings this way. Proceed just as if you were making the tiramisu in the sheet pan, starting with a piece of soaked Savoiardi in the bottom of the glass and layering it up with the cream.

4. Spread half of the mascarpone cream, half of the shaved chocolate, and half of the chopped pistachios, and repeat to make another layer: the rest of the mascarpone cream, the rest of the white chocolate, and the rest of the pistachios. Refrigerate for at least 2 hours before slicing/serving.

5. You can also freeze the tiramisu for up to 2 months and let it thaw at room temperature for 20 minutes before serving.

PISTACHIO BUTTER

1 cup (5.6 oz/160 g) unsalted raw pistachios

3 tablespoon melted cocoa butter or flavorless organic vegetable oil

2 pinches of salt

Put the pistachios in a (preferably powerful) food processor or blender, and blend until a paste forms. If using cocoa butter, melt it in a glass or metal bowl over a pot of boiling water, making sure the bowl does not touch the water (or use a double boiler). When the blender is starting to have some difficulties processing the pistachio butter, add half of the oil and keep processing, stopping every minute or so to scrape down the sides. Then add the remaining oil and keep processing, stopping every minute to scrape down the sides, until the pistachio butter starts to get really creamy and loose and you do not need to scrape down the sides as often. The whole process will take 10 to 20 minutes, depending on how powerful your processor is. The pinches of salt are essential to bring out the flavor of the pistachios and, even though the pistachio butter might seem a little salty, it does wonders when used in sweets.

AS SOON AS THE WEATHER STARTS GETTING REALLY COLD, my mom inevitably pulls out her wooden pasta board, which she also uses for baking, and says, "Time to make cantucci." You'll also find that the windows of most bakeries and pastry shops in north and central Italy are lined with basketfuls of these little almond-studded biscotti, their sweet, anise-y scent whiffing out of the doors and drawing passersby inside. This is a hundred-year-old tried-and-true family recipe for cantucci, for which the recipe can vary slightly outside of Tuscany (some add butter, some do not, some use hazelnuts in lieu of almonds, and so on). Most people who have tried them say that they are the best version they've ever tasted! And I agree. They are quite crispy, so enjoy them dipped in sweet wine, such as vin santo—or just in tea or coffee.

CLASSIC BISCOTTI
Tuscan "Cantucci"

MAKES ABOUT 50 COOKIES

2 cups (8.8 oz/250 g) whole-wheat flour, plus more for dusting

2 cups (8.8 oz/250 g) white wheat or spelt flour

1 teaspoon baking powder

1 teaspoon baking soda

1½ cups (8.8 oz/250 g) packed dark brown sugar, plus more for sprinkling

4 eggs, 3 whole and 1 separated

2 heaping tablespoons honey

2 tablespoons anise-flavored liqueur, such as Sambuca (optional; substitute 1 teaspoon ground anise seeds if you don't have Sambuca)

½ teaspoon anise seeds, crushed to a powder

2 teaspoons vanilla extract

Grated zest of ½ medium lemon

1¼ cups (7 oz/200 g) mixed almonds and hazelnuts, or a combination of the nuts

1. Preheat the oven to 350°F/180°C.

2. Put the flours, baking powder, baking soda, brown sugar, whole eggs, egg white, honey, anise liqueur, anise seeds, vanilla, and lemon zest in a food processor and process until combined. You can also mix in a large bowl with a wooden spoon. You should end up with a very sticky dough, difficult to manage but not too liquidy or loose. If the dough is too tough, add a splash of water. Add the nuts. Add the chocolate chips, raisins, and/or other dried fruits (if using), and mix well again.

3. Line a baking sheet with wax paper and divide the dough into five pieces. Flour your hands and shape each section into a 1½-inch-wide (4 cm) log and place them on the baking sheet. The logs will expand while they bake, so make sure to leave at least 2 inches (5 cm) of space between them. Brush them well with the leftover yolk from the separated egg and sprinkle granulated sugar on top. Bake the logs for 20 to 25 minutes, or until brown (baking time will depend on your oven—start keeping an eye on the logs around the 15-minute mark). When you take them out of the oven, they will be soft and will have

ingredients and recipe continue

½ cup (100 g) of any of the following: chocolate chips; raisins, soaked and squeezed out; any other dried fruit (optional)

Granulated sugar, to sprinkle on top

cracked slightly on top. Using a serrated knife, slice them immediately into ½-inch (1.5 cm) slices, using a tea towel to protect your hands from the heat. Spread them on the baking sheet, turn off the oven, and return them to the oven until completely cool. Serve once cool, and store them in a sealed cookie tin or in an airtight container. Enjoy dipped in dessert wine, coffee, or even just water alone. They are also delicious just as is!

TIP: If you prefer a softer cookie, add ¼ cup (50 ml) vegetable oil or 3 tablespoons butter to the dough while kneading.

SPRING

As we drove two hours from home along the only road that cuts the immense fields around the town of Castelluccio, a bouquet of quiet and pretty houses that sits on a hill in the middle of a valley in Umbria, we wondered aloud when the flowers would appear. In that valley, sloping below the Umbrian mountains, lay the largest green field I had ever seen. In the height of spring, it would be painted in strands of purple, blue, red, and white. "Spring is late here," said my boyfriend. "Or did we arrive early?"

But you know it is spring before it is actually spring: When the first buds start popping on the branches of almond and cherry trees, even if they are still covered in snow, it is spring. When the days get longer, even if the grass is still covered in frost, it is spring.

Late March stretches itself awake lazily, touching everything like a lover with cold feet. The awakening is sudden, and one day, while bike-riding or taking a stroll along the fields, you see all the fava beans plants, cherry trees, and plum trees in full bloom. The air and the ground start to fill with so many swirling, falling things: petals, pollen, whole flowers, insects. Sometimes, when the poplar trees that line our roads let their white fluffy pollen fall, it feels like walking through a scenery of summery winter, as though snow has miraculously managed to linger on in the warmer weather.

Spring is a season full of *wabi*, which, in Japanese culture, refers to the delicate elegance of impermanent things: fleeting beauty, intense and short lasting. Spring's flowers and produce last only a handful of weeks—sometimes only days. The moments of spring are precious moments to witness, savor, and touch with all of our senses. Fava beans will be gone before you can even come up with anything creative to do with them, and fresh peas are just a green sparkle appearing and disappearing like flickering lights on the market shelves. The beautiful almond and cherry petals will be falling in a matter of hours, and all that will be left is their blushing blossoms on the ground, washed by April rains. In Italy, Easter celebrations are a major event and, much like at Christmastime, we prepare a bounty of festive and traditional dishes. The symbolism of death and rebirth at Easter echoes the *wabi* of spring. Each spring, I am in awe of the miracle of life renewed.

That day, driving outside of Castelluccio, we turned a corner and suddenly the most springlike of sceneries unfolded before us: an immense field of golden flowers. It was the prettiest, most majestic landscape I had ever seen. We stopped the car and dove into the flowers like kids in a playground.

We were not that early, after all.

RECIPES

Mains

Stinging Nettle Soup with Cannellini Beans (V/GF)

Chickpea Crespelle with Spring Vegetable Ragù (V/GF)

Green "Strozzapreti" with Cherry Tomatoes & Aromatic Sauce (V)

Vegetarian Carbonara with Zucchini & Asparagus

Farrotto with Wild Asparagus (V)

Erbazzone, Spelt Pizza Pie Stuffed with Wild Greens

Stuffed Artichokes with Peas (V/GF)

Veggie-Loaded Chickpea Cakes with Pecorino (GF)

Stuffed Frittata Roll with Spinach & Arugula Mediterranean Pesto (GF)

Sides & Salads

New Potatoes with Parsley Dressing

Spring Pasticcio with Leeks & Cipollini (Veganizable/GF)

"La Vignarola," Braised Fava Beans, Lettuce, Artichokes & Peas (V/GF)

"La Bagiana," Fava Bean Stew (V/GF)

Braised Artichokes, "Romagna-Style" (V)

Sweets & Desserts

Coconut Caramel Panna Cotta with Chocolate (V/GF)

Almond Crostata with Ricotta & Jam Filling (GF)

My Nonna's Prune Cake with Dried Fruit (V)

Almond Amaretto Cake with Visciole Cherries (GF)

WHAT AMAZES ME most about country life is that food is everywhere if you learn to recognize it. When spring approaches, bushes upon bushes of wild herbs like nettles and dandelions sprout in every field, ready to be picked. Among these, baby nettles are some of the tastiest. Wearing gloves, my mom and I pick the tender sprouts, filling our bags with only the greenest and most fragrant ones. Back at home, we wash our finds in our marble sink, chattering about our plans to use the herbs in pasta, soups, condiments, and pesto. For this recipe, I took my inspiration from a simple yet wonderful soup I had in a quaint restaurant inside the castle of Gradara. That meal was years ago, yet the memory has stayed with me.

STINGING NETTLE SOUP
With Cannellini Beans

SERVES 2 TO 3

2 tablespoons extra-virgin olive oil, plus more for drizzling

1 small onion, minced

1 shallot, finely sliced (or substitute with more onion)

4 cups (4.2 oz/120 g) packed raw nettles (or mix with spinach and other greens if you can't find enough), finely chopped

½ cup (3.5 oz/100 g) dry cannellini beans, soaked overnight, or 1 cup (250 ml) cooked cannellini, rinsed

½ cup (3.5 oz/100 g) whole farro (or spelt), soaked overnight (see Note)

6 cups (1½ l) Vegetable Stock (page 32)

1 teaspoon salt

¼ teaspoon pepper

1 heaping tablespoon Pesto Ligure (page 40), to finish

1. Place the olive oil in a medium pot. Add the onion and shallot. Sauté over very low heat for about 10 minutes, until the alliums are translucent and start to turn golden in color. Add a bit of water if they stick.

2. Add the nettles to the pot when the alliums are ready. Cook the nettles for about 2 minutes, until wilted. Then add the cannellini and farro. Cover with the stock, add a pinch of salt and pepper, and cook, half-covered, for 1 to 1½ hours, until the farro and beans are ready. (If using cooked beans, do not add them at the start—just add them with 15 minutes of cooking time remaining.)

3. Adjust salt and pepper to taste and finish, if you wish, with some Classic Pesto or with some more extra-virgin olive oil per bowl. Serve hot, as a one-pot meal or with a salad.

CRESPELLE ARE THE ITALIAN VERSION OF FRENCH CREPES, but they are only used in savory preparations. They are served at Easter and other festivities along with dishes such as lasagna and other pasta bakes. The ingredients in this recipe reflect the spring season: eggs from the surplus that hens begin to lay, incredible green veggies just starting to appear in the garden, and the fresh ricotta that farmers begin making promptly in March. You can make cannelloni with any kind of flour, but in this version I use chickpea flour for its nutty taste and to make the meal gluten-free.

CHICKPEA CRESPELLE
With Spring Vegetable Ragù

....

SERVES 4; MAKES 8 CRESPELLE

....

1 recipe Spring Ragù Sauce
 (page 39)

For the crespelle:

½ cup (2.8 oz/80 g) chickpea flour

1 cup (250 ml) goat's milk (see Notes)

2 large eggs

¼ cup (50 ml) water

½ teaspoon salt

Oil or butter, for the pan

For the ricotta filling:

1¼ cups (300 g) creamy ricotta
 (see Notes)

¼ cup (1 oz/30 g) grated pecorino
 or hard seasoned goat cheese,
 or more to taste

¼ teaspoon grated nutmeg

Pinch of salt

Pinch of pepper

1. Prepare the ragù according to the recipe on page 39. Divide the ragù and puree half of it.

2. Make the crespelle: Place the flour in a medium bowl and add the milk a little at a time, mixing it in with a whisk to avoid lumps. In a separate large bowl, beat the eggs with a fork until uniform in color. Add them to the flour along with the water. You should end up with a smooth, somewhat liquid batter. Set aside in the fridge for at least 1 hour.

3. Heat a nonstick 8-inch (20-cm) pan over high heat and, once hot, reduce the heat to medium. Add a little oil to the pan, enough to very lightly coat the bottom, and add a generous ¼ cup (50 ml) of the batter. With a spatula, swirl the batter around to fully coat the pan and cook for about 1 minute before turning it over, very carefully, with a spatula. Cook for 1 minute more. Remove from the pan and set aside on separate dish. Repeat with another ¼-cup (50-ml) portion of the batter. The batter should make eight crespelle.

4. Make the ricotta filling: In a medium bowl, place the ricotta, pecorino, nutmeg, salt, and pepper. Mix well. The filling should not need much salt and pepper, but adjust the salt, pepper, and cheese to your liking.

To assemble:

Oil, for the baking pan

More grated cheese

Extra-virgin olive oil, for drizzling

Finely chopped scallions

5. To assemble: Preheat the oven to broil. Lightly oil a 9 × 13-inch (22 × 33-cm) baking pan. On a separate work surface, spread a heaping teaspoon of the ricotta filling and a couple teaspoons of the ragù puree in the upper half of each crepe. Roll them into a cigar shape. Repeat for all the crepes and lay them in the baking pan. Be sure they have enough room so that they don't touch. Top with the un-pureed ragù, a little more grated cheese, and a small drizzle of olive oil. Broil them just until the cheese is completely melted and the top gets golden and bubbling.

6. Serve with finely chopped scallions on top.

NOTES: I prefer using goat cheese ricotta for this recipe, as its taste really makes me think of spring and Easter. It's also very creamy. I don't recommend using sheep's milk ricotta, as it tends to release more liquid. You can use ricotta from cow's milk, but make sure to use the best quality you can find, since it will be a dominant flavor.

You can prepare the ragù, crespelle, and filling a day in advance and assemble everything right before you need it. The crespelle will keep for 3 days stacked in the fridge.

STROZZAPRETI LITERALLY MEANS "CHOKE THE PRIEST." There are several theories about the origins of the curious name of this twisty pasta, but my favorite is that it was a special pasta that village women once prepared for the town priest when he came to visit, causing their husbands to feel so jealous, they wished the priest would choke as he ate.

Strozzapreti are so wonderful to cook with because their twisty shape catches any sauce perfectly. This pasta is a specialty of the Emilia-Romagna region of Italy, where part of my family is from. It is worth taking the time to make the pasta yourself—hand-rolling it is half the fun!

GREEN "STROZZAPRETI"
With Cherry Tomatoes & Aromatic Sauce

SERVES 4

For the pasta:

1 cup (4.5 oz/130 g) white spelt flour

½ cup (2.8 oz/80 g) semolina flour (or white flour)

1 cup (5.3 oz/150 g) whole-wheat flour, preferably stone-milled

½ cup (125 ml) cooked greens (nettles, dandelion, spinach . . .), excess water tightly squeezed out

For the sauce:

⅓ cup (75 ml) olive oil

2 tablespoons fresh rosemary, finely minced

1 tablespoon fresh marjoram leaves

½ medium onion, minced

One 3-inch (7.5 cm) piece of celery, minced

1 pound (450 g) ripe cherry tomatoes, halved

About 6 basil leaves, or more to taste

Pinch of salt, plus more if needed

¼ teaspoon pepper

Coarse salt, for the pasta water

1. Make the pasta: Place the white spelt flour, semolina flour, whole-wheat flour, and greens in a food processor and pulse to combine. Very slowly, add water 1 tablespoon at a time until the flour and greens come together in a dough (you might need anywhere from ¼ cup [50 ml] to ½ cup [125 ml], or more). Scrape the dough out of the processor and knead it on a work surface until the dough is smooth. Put it in the fridge to rest for 30 minutes or up to overnight.

2. Roll out the dough, making sure it is not too thin (setting 7 on a pasta machine). Cut it into ½-inch-long (1.5 cm) strips, as if you were making tagliatelle (follow the instructions on page 56). Then rub the end of a strip between the palms of your hands to create a twisty shape, as you can see in the photos on page 58. Break the strozzapreti with your hands into 2-inch (5-cm) pieces and drop the pieces onto a well-floured rimmed baking sheet. Repeat until you run out of strips.

3. Make the sauce: Heat the olive oil in a large pan over low heat. Add the rosemary and marjoram and cook for about 2 minutes, until aromatic. (The smell should fill your whole kitchen!) Add the onion and celery and sauté for about 5 minutes, until the onion is translucent. Then add the cherry tomatoes. Cook, covered, for about 15 minutes more, until the

recipe continues

NOTE: You can prepare the dough and sauce the day before.

mixture is soft and juicy. Add a pinch of salt, mix, and let the sauce reduce, uncovered, for 3 minutes more.

4. Bring a pot with plenty of water to a rolling boil, adding salt in the proportion of 1 scant teaspoon for every 4 cups (1 l) of water. Once boiling, begin to heat the sauce as well in a separate saucepan over medium-low heat. Dump the strozzapreti into the boiling water. Cook for 3 minutes and drain the strozzapreti with a handheld colander and then add it straight into the pan, letting some of the pasta water drip in. Bring the heat to high and mix for about 2 minutes, until heated through and well coated with sauce. Adjust the salt and pepper if necessary. Serve immediately.

Shaping strozzapreti pasta (plain strozzapreti pictured)

I DO NOT THINK there is another population in this world who can argue over a recipe like the Italians. We have strong opinions on all things food, but there is one dish that triggers more arguments than any other: carbonara. Pancetta or guanciale? Cream or no cream? And how much pepper? Still, there are two things we all agree on: The pasta should be tossed with the sauce and pasta water to make the carbonara creamy and not scrambly, and, of course, we agree that, no matter how it is prepared, carbonara is delicious.

Here, I use neither pancetta nor guanciale, but the cheese and eggs paired with asparagus make for a carbonara that is just as delicious. It will not make you miss the original, but should you ever make this for an Italian, be sure you don't say that you are serving carbonara. You might be stuck in an argument for a while!

VEGETARIAN CARBONARA
With Zucchini & Asparagus

SERVES 4

¼ cup (60 ml) olive oil

1 medium onion or leek (7 oz/200 g), thinly sliced

2 small zucchini (7 oz/200 g), halved and thinly sliced

16 asparagus spears (7 oz/200 g), trimmed of the hard stalk and thinly sliced

1½ teaspoons salt, plus 2 pinches for the pasta water

10 ounces (270 g) whole-wheat or spelt spaghetti or paccheri

2 large eggs plus 2 large egg yolks

⅓ cup (1.7 oz/50 g) grated pecorino or Grana cheese, plus more to finish

1 teaspoon pepper, plus more to finish

1. Place the olive oil and onion in a medium-large pan and sauté over medium heat, stirring often, for about 5 minutes, until the onion is translucent. Add the zucchini, asparagus, and 1 teaspoon salt and cook while stirring for 5 minutes more. Add ½ cup (50 ml) water, cover, and cook for about 15 minutes, until almost all of the water is gone. All the vegetables should be soft at this point. If they are not, add another splash of water and cook until tender. When the vegetables are cooked, uncover, stir, and let the remaining water evaporate completely.

2. Bring a large pot of water to a boil over high heat, then add coarse salt in the proportion of 1 scant teaspoon for every 4 cups (1 l) water. Boil the pasta according to the package instructions, but drain it 2 minutes before the end of the cooking time. Reserve about ½ cup (125 ml) of the pasta water.

3. Meanwhile, place the whole eggs and yolks in a medium bowl and whisk them with the cheese, the remaining ½ teaspoon of salt, and the pepper.

recipe continues

NOTE: When cool, this pasta might curdle up a bit. Do not reheat in a microwave, or the egg will curdle. Reheat gently in a pan, adding 2 tablespoons of water to make it creamy again.

4. Add the drained pasta to the pan and toss it well with the vegetable mixture over low heat for 1 minute. Remove from the heat, pour in the egg mixture, add 2 tablespoons of the reserved pasta water, and toss to coat with a fork and spoon: The egg mixture should form a cream with the starch in the pasta water, and it will cook with the residual heat of the pan and hot pasta. Use more pasta water if it seems too dry. Place the pan over medium-low heat and let the sauce thicken for 1 minute, stirring constantly. Do not let the egg curdle. Serve immediately with extra pepper and a sprinkling of extra grated cheese.

FARROTTO, RISOTTO, AND ORZOTTO are traditionally finished with cheese. After the heavy dishes of winter, the last thing I want is more hard, seasoned cheese, so instead I like to use bright, tasty spices. These creamy, comforting preparations take to spices well and are perfect soul food when the season starts turning warm. Here I use vibrant, healthy turmeric to give farrotto a tasty and colorful complement to the recipe. You could use saffron instead, which always works well with asparagus, and if you absolutely want cheese, try a crumbling of sheep's or goat's milk ricotta, which is easier to digest and perfectly in season. Do add the pepper—it enhances the absorption of all of turmeric's healthy nutrients!

Wild asparagus is commonly foraged all around the countryside and is usually thinner and longer than normal asparagus. If you cannot find it, use regular asparagus. If you prefer, substitute orzo or risotto rice instead of the farro.

FARROTTO
With Wild Asparagus

SERVES 2

2 tablespoons extra-virgin olive oil

4 medium shallots, thinly sliced

About 30 wild asparagus spears (14 oz/400 g), or about 20 regular asparagus, cleaned and sliced into thin rounds

1¼ cups (8.8 oz/250 g) farro, hulled or pearled

½ teaspoon salt or more to taste

¼ teaspoon pepper, plus more for finishing

½ cup (125 ml) white wine

About 4 cups (1 l) Vegetable Stock (page 32), plus more as needed

½ cup (125 ml) unsweetened almond milk or regular milk

1 teaspoon ground turmeric (optional)

2 tablespoons fresh parsley, finely chopped, or more to taste and for finishing

Heat the olive oil in a large pan over medium heat. Add the shallots and sauté for about 15 minutes, until golden. Add the asparagus. Cook while stirring for 2 minutes, then add the farro and toast it for 1 minute. Add the salt and pepper, then deglaze with the wine. Raise the heat to high and let the wine bubble off for 30 seconds, then cover the farro with half the stock. Cook for about 10 minutes, until the stock is absorbed. Add the remaining stock and, after 20 minutes, stir in the almond milk. As the farro absorbs the liquid, you might need to add a little more stock. Stir every now and then, adding more broth as it is absorbed. Pearled farro will take about 40 minutes to cook, while whole farro may take more than 1 hour. If using, add the turmeric 5 minutes before the barley is ready and adjust the seasoning with salt and pepper. Right before serving, add the parsley and stir to mix. Serve immediately with a simple garden salad.

THIS RECIPE HAILS FROM the Emilia side of Emilia-Romagna, where residents definitely love their pork. Emilia is the birthplace of prosciutto, and it is not uncommon to see cold cuts and salami hanging from every shop window. Like most recipes from this region, the Erbazzone dough is traditionally made with lard and the greens are cooked in pancetta and pork fat. This delicious vegetarian version uses olive oil instead of lard, and pizza dough makes for a much lighter dish that is still incredibly comforting. It will fill your whole kitchen with the smell of cheese pizza.

ERBAZZONE
Spelt Pizza Pie Stuffed with Wild Greens

MAKES ONE 10-INCH (25-CM) PIE

3 tablespoons olive oil, plus more for the pan and for brushing

3 or 4 garlic cloves, crushed

1 large onion, finely sliced

1½ pounds (700 g) mixed wild greens (beet greens, dandelion greens, spinach, nettles, chard . . .)

1 teaspoon salt

½ teaspoon pepper

1 cup (8.8 oz/250 g) fresh ricotta cheese

3 to 5 tablespoons grated pecorino cheese

½ recipe pizza dough from Quick Pizza (page 46)

1. Place the olive oil in a large pan over medium-high heat and add the garlic. Sauté for 2 to 3 minutes, until aromatic. Add the onion, reduce the heat to low, and cook while stirring for 10 minutes, or until the onion is golden. Should the onion stick to the pan, add a splash of water. Discard the garlic.

2. Raise the heat to medium and add the greens, salt, and pepper. Cook while stirring for about 10 minutes, until the greens are completely wilted and almost melting. Let cool for 10 minutes, then stir in the ricotta and pecorino.

3. In the meantime, preheat the oven to 475°F (245°C) and lightly oil a 10-inch (25 cm) pie pan with a little olive oil.

4. Divide the pizza dough into two parts. Roll each into a 12-inch (30 cm) circle, and place one circle in the pan. Spread the herb and ricotta filling evenly, brush the edges with olive oil, and cover with the other circle of dough, pinching the edges together as when you make pie. Brush the top with a little olive oil, and bake for about 40 minutes, until the top is golden. Check the pie at around the 30-minute mark, as it tends to burn easily past this point.

5. Slice it and serve hot. This pie freezes beautifully: Once baked, you can freeze it whole or presliced, then thaw it for 2 hours and reheat it in the oven.

THIS DISH IS INSPIRED BY a traditional recipe from Apulia, on the southern coast of the Adriatic Sea. Back in the early 1900s, many farmers in Italy were poor, but farmers from the South seemed to be exceptionally so. The lack of meat created a regional cuisine that is made up largely of the South's beautiful, sun-kissed produce. This artichoke dish is a great example of a typical southern dish. The traditional recipe calls for stale bread to stuff the artichokes, but you can always use the Millet & Rice Stuffing for Vegetables (page 209) for a gluten-free twist.

I love how the artichokes easily give in to the fork once soft and cooked, and the sweet aroma of garlicky oil hits your nostrils. The Mediterranean flavor of the artichokes and parsley fills every mouthful.

STUFFED ARTICHOKES
With Peas

SERVES 6 AS A SIDE, 3 AS A MAIN

Five ½-inch (1.5 cm) slices of crusty, stale sourdough whole-wheat bread (or about ⅓ recipe for Millet & Rice Stuffing for Vegetables, page 209)

¾ cup (175 ml) milk, regular or nondairy

1 garlic clove, finely minced

2 tablespoons fresh parsley, finely chopped

1 teaspoon salt, plus 2 pinches

½ teaspoon freshly ground black pepper

3 tablespoons grated Grana or pecorino cheese (skip if vegan)

6 large artichokes, trimmed

5 tablespoons (75 ml) olive oil

1 large shallot, finely minced

1½ cups (7.7 oz/220 g) peas, fresh or frozen

½ cup (125 ml) white wine

½ cup (125 ml) water

1 tablespoon finely chopped pine nuts or almonds

1. Tear the bread slices into pieces and put them in a large baking pan with high sides (try to be sure the bread pieces do not overlap). Pour the milk over the bread and soak for 5 minutes. Then squeeze out the excess milk and transfer the bread to a bowl. Mix in the garlic, parsley, ½ teaspoon of the salt, the pepper, and the cheese (if using). Set aside.

2. Trim the artichokes and open them in the middle, then scoop out the middle part with a teaspoon. Stuff each with the millet or bread mixture.

3. Put the olive oil in an ovenproof pan or casserole dish along with the shallots. Sauté the shallots over medium-low heat for about 5 minutes, until the shallots turn translucent. Add the peas and remaining ½ teaspoon salt and cook while stirring for 5 minutes. Add the artichokes, stuffed-side up. Add the wine to the pan, along with the water. Cover and cook for about 45 minutes, until the artichokes are soft.

4. Preheat the oven to 400°F (205°C). Once the artichokes are ready, uncover the pan and sprinkle the artichokes with the chopped nuts. Transfer the pan with the artichokes to the oven and bake for 15 minutes, until the top part gets crispy. (Alternatively, you can finish them for 5 minutes in the broiler.)

CHICKPEA FLOUR IS THE MAIN INGREDIENT of a Sicilian dish called panelle. To make panelle, you spread a thin layer of batter on a surface until dry, then you cut it into pieces and deep-fry it. It is traditionally eaten in a sandwich. Panelle was my inspiration the first time I created these chickpea pancakes. They are not deep-fried and they are packed with vegetables, but I bet they would be amazing between two slices of whole sourdough bread. They are definitely delicious on their own. This recipe is gluten-free, and you can make it dairy-free, too, if you wish. Feel free to customize with any kind of vegetable you like.

VEGGIE-LOADED CHICKPEA PANCAKES
With Pecorino

MAKES TEN 2-INCH (5-CM) CAKES

For the batter:

2 cups (6.3 oz/220 g) chickpea flour

1 teaspoon salt

1¼ cups (300 ml) water

For the vegetables:

2 tablespoons olive oil, plus more

1 large onion, thinly sliced

1 medium leek, thinly sliced

5 spring onions, thinly sliced

3 medium shallots, thinly sliced

2 small zucchini, halved and thinly sliced

6 zucchini flowers, thinly sliced

½ teaspoon salt

Pinch of pepper

¼ cup chopped fresh parsley

¼ cup chopped fresh basil

3 small sprigs of fresh marjoram

¼ cup (1 oz/30 g) grated pecorino cheese (substitute 1 tablespoon nutritional yeast for vegan variation)

1. **Make the batter:** Put the chickpea flour and salt in a medium bowl and slowly whisk in the water, making sure there are no lumps. Whisk until the batter thickens, cover, and refrigerate for at least 30 minutes for best results, or overnight.

2. **Prepare the vegetables:** Heat the olive oil in a large pan over medium-high heat and add the onion, leek, spring onions, and shallots. Sauté for about 10 minutes, until translucent and golden. Add the zucchini, zucchini flowers, salt, pepper, parsley, basil, and marjoram (if using). Cover and cook for about 15 minutes, until the vegetables are soft, checking every now and then. If the vegetables dry out too much, add 2 tablespoons water.

3. Once the vegetables are ready, scrape the mixture into the bowl with the batter and mix to combine well. Add the pecorino and mix.

4. Heat a nonstick pan or cast-iron skillet over medium heat and lightly oil it. Add a scant ¼ cup (50 ml) of the batter per pancake, cover, and cook for 1½ minutes. Flip the cakes and cook for 1 minute more on the other side, or until golden brown.

5. Serve with some Pesto Ligure (page 40), a fresh green salad on the side for a light lunch, or "La Vignarola" (page 172).

MY FAVORITE STORIES FROM WHEN my mom was young and worked as a hotel cook are about the dishes they used to prepare. One dish that always made an appearance at the buffet was a frittata roll. Back then, it was stuffed with ham and cheese and served with mayonnaise—a crowd-pleasing but very heavy dish. I decided to take the stuffed frittata roll out of the eighties and make it more modern. This tasty dairy-free version is great to serve at parties or to eat as a cold lunch when the warm weather starts to kick in.

STUFFED FRITTATA ROLL
With Spinach & Arugula Mediterranean Pesto

SERVES 8 AS AN APPETIZER, 4 AS A MAIN

For the pesto:

2 cups (60 g) packed arugula

½ cup (2 oz/55 g) pitted olives

3 halves sun-dried tomatoes in olive oil

1 tablespoon capers, rinsed

1 garlic clove

10 fresh basil leaves

½ teaspoon salt

¼ cup (50 ml) extra-virgin olive oil

For the spinach filling:

2 teaspoons olive oil

1 garlic clove, crushed

1 pound (450 g) fresh spinach, chopped

1 teaspoon salt

Pinch of pepper

2 tablespoons water

For the frittata:

6 large eggs

½ teaspoon salt

¼ teaspoon pepper

¼ cup (50 ml) unsweetened nondairy milk or regular milk

1. Make the pesto: Combine the arugula, olives, sun-dried tomatoes, capers, garlic, basil, and salt in a blender or food processor and process until a paste forms. Slowly add the oil and blend until creamy (a little less if you prefer a chunky pesto).

2. Make the spinach filling: Heat the olive oil in a medium pan over medium heat and add the garlic. Sauté until aromatic, then add the spinach, salt, pepper, and water. Cook, covered, for about 2 minutes, until the spinach is wilted. Uncover and sauté about 5 minutes more, until all liquid is gone. Discard the garlic.

3. Make the frittata: Preheat the oven to 375°F (190°C). Line a 9 × 13-inch (22 × 33-cm) casserole dish with wax paper.

4. Whisk the eggs, salt, pepper, and milk together in a medium bowl with a fork until well combined. Pour the mixture into the casserole dish and bake for about 15 minutes, until cooked through and puffed. Let it cool slightly, but not completely— make sure it is warm when assembling.

5. To assemble: Remove the frittata from the casserole dish and lay it on a work surface. Spread it evenly with the pesto and then the spinach. Delicately roll the frittata into a log. Lay it with the edges down, and let it cool completely before cutting. Cut into 1-inch-thick (2.5-cm) slices and serve cold with any side of vegetables.

IN EARLY SPRING WE COLLECT OUR NEW, thumb-sized potatoes from the ground in large vats, which then sit impatiently in the back of the house, waiting to be turned into something delicious. Often we use them in this salad—it's frequently on my grandma's Sunday table in the springtime. These days, I eat more sweet potatoes than white potatoes, and I can tell you that this dressing works wonderfully with sweet potatoes, too (or on any vegetable, really). But the original recipe is a very classic side dish.

NEW POTATOES
With Parsley Dressing

SERVES 6 AS A SIDE

2 pounds (900 g) new potatoes, russet red potatoes, or sweet potatoes

1 large white or red onion, finely sliced

For the dressing:

½ cup (20 g) loosely packed parsley, finely chopped

1 tablespoon capers, rinsed

¼ cup (60 ml) white wine vinegar

1 tablespoon Balsamic Glaze (page 50) (or regular balsamic if you cannot find the thick one)

4 to 5 tablespoons (60 to 75 ml) extra-virgin olive oil

1 teaspoon salt or to taste

½ teaspoon pepper

1. Fill a large pot of water, add the potatoes, and bring to a boil over high heat. Cook for 15 to 30 minutes, until the potatoes are tender (cooking time will depend on the size and freshness of the potatoes). To test for doneness, pierce a potato with a toothpick or a fork—it should pierce the potato easily all the way to the center. Drain the potatoes and let them cool until they are easy to handle.

2. Make the dressing: In a food processor or blender, place the parsley, capers, vinegar, balsamic glaze, salt, and pepper and process. While processing, add 4 tablespoons (60 ml) of the olive oil in a thin stream. Add up to 1 tablespoon more, per your preference.

3. Peel the potatoes with your hands and cut them into bite-size pieces. Toss in a bowl with the onion and dressing.

FOR AN "ITALIAN POTATO SALAD" VARIATION: Stir a finely chopped-up hard-boiled egg into the dressing and chop the potatoes into smaller pieces. Serve with other steamed or boiled vegetables for a delicious meal.

FOR A SUMMER
VARIATION: Mix in ½ cup
halved cherry tomatoes before
adding the vegetables to the oven.

WHEN THE SPRING GARDEN REACHES ITS PEAK in April to May, we find ourselves with basketfuls of fresh alliums and green vegetables. Here's a wonderful way to take advantage of all the best spring onions in one Sunday casserole. It is super simple to make, yet looks and tastes like a million dollars. It makes a satisfying side dish for a Sunday meal, but it is also delicious on its own with some boiled grains or legumes. Make it with regular or vegan Béchamel Sauce (page 35)—either way is delicious.

SPRING PASTICCIO
With Leeks & Cipollini

SERVES 4 AS A SIDE

5 tablespoons (75 ml) olive oil

3 medium leeks, cleaned and thinly sliced

4 medium cipollini or shallots, thinly sliced

1½ teaspoons salt,

1 small head puntarelle (substitute any other leafy green if you cannot find any), cut into 1-inch pieces

Pepper to taste

Variation 1:

⅓ cup (75 ml) Crumb Topping "Alla Romagnola" (page 49)

Variation 2:

½ recipe Béchamel Sauce or vegan Béchamel Sauce (page 35)

3 tablespoons grated Grana or Parmesan cheese (or nutritional yeast to keep it vegan)

2 heaping tablespoons almond slivers or finely chopped pistachios

1. Heat 3 tablespoons of the olive oil in a medium pan over medium heat and add the leeks and cipollini. Sauté on medium-low, half-covered, for about 10 minutes, stirring often, until golden. Add 1 teaspoon of the salt and 2 tablespoons water. Cook, covered, for 5 minutes more. Uncover and cook for 5 minutes more, until any leftover liquid has evaporated.

2. Heat the remaining 2 tablespoons olive oil in another medium pan and add the puntarelle, the remaining ½ teaspoon salt, and pepper to taste. Stir and add 3 tablespoons water, then cook, covered, for about 15 minutes, until the vegetables are softened. Uncover and let any liquid evaporate completely.

3. Preheat the oven 400°F (205°C).

4. Transfer the vegetables to an 11 × 7 × 2-inch (28 × 18 × 5-cm) baking dish.

For variation 1: Toss the vegetables with half the crumb topping and spread evenly in the baking dish. Top with the remaining crumbs and half of the slivered almonds. Bake for 10 minutes, toss the vegetables with a spoon, spread out evenly again, top with the remaining almonds, and bake for 10 minutes more, or until golden and crisped up.

For variation 2: Mix the vegetables with béchamel sauce and finish with the cheese and slivered almonds.

5. Bake for 30 minutes, or until golden and bubbling on top.

AS SOON AS THE FIRST PEARLY-WHITE BLOOMS APPEAR ON THE FAVA PLANTS in the garden, I think of "La Vignarola." This Roman recipe features a panful of mixed healthy green vegetables, simply sautéed with garlic and wine. Fava beans, which are an important part of Roman cuisine, are the real protagonists of this dish. They look like green jewels in the pan. This is a protein-loaded vegan side dish that can be turned into a main meal with the addition of a whole grain.

"LA VIGNAROLA"

Braised Fava Beans, Lettuce, Artichokes & Peas

SERVES 4 AS A SIDE, 2 AS A MAIN

½ lemon

5 purple artichokes, or 3 if using large Globe artichokes

3 tablespoons olive oil

1 large onion, thinly sliced

2 pounds (900 g) fresh fava beans, shelled

1 cup (5.3 oz/150 g) shelled peas, fresh or frozen

1 teaspoon salt

Pepper

1. Prepare a bowl of cold water, squeeze in the lemon juice, then add the already-squeezed ½ lemon as well. Remove the tough outer leaves of the artichokes and, using a teaspoon, open the artichokes up and scoop out the hearts to remove the furry part. Cut off the tips and finely slice them, adding them directly to the bowl with the acidulated water.

2. Heat the olive oil in a large pan over medium-high heat and add the onion. Sauté for 2 minutes. Then add 2 tablespoons water and sauté for 5 minutes more. Add the drained artichokes and ¼ cup (50 ml) more water. Cook, half-covered, for 5 minutes. Add the fava beans, peas, salt, pepper to taste, and an additional ½ cup (125 ml) water and cook, half-covered, for 15 minutes, stirring every now and then. Uncover and cook for 5 to 10 minutes more, or until the water has almost completely evaporated. All of the vegetables should be tender (depending on how fresh they are, they might take more or less time to cook).

NOTE: To make it a one-bowl meal, serve with brown rice or any other grain. You can also use this as a base to make a risotto, farrotto, or orzotto: Just add your grain of choice after you have sautéed all of the vegetables for 5 minutes, then follow the instructions for making Pumpkin Orzotto (page 72) or Risotto with Radicchio & Walnuts (page 117).

FOR A SOUP VARIATION: You can turn this into a soup by adding enough water to cover the fava beans by 1½ inches (4 cm). Simmer over low heat for 30 to 35 minutes. For a smooth soup, puree in a blender. For a creamy yet chunky soup, puree half of the mixture and return it to the pot.

To serve, place a slice of toasted garlicky bread in the bottom of each bowl and ladle the soup on top.

THIS SIDE DISH OF FAVA BEANS, which hails from central Italy, is best scooped up with garlicky bruschetta. I found several versions bearing the same name: Some feature chard and some feature tomatoes. I decided to go with the tomato version that has always been made in my home. Fava beans and tomato passata are a great pairing—they create a dish that is tasty and incredibly full of nutritional benefits. Fava beans, a longtime spring staple for Italian farmers and always paired with pecorino by shepherds, are rich in plant-based protein and fiber. You can puree the fava beans to make a great dip as well!

"LA BAGIANA"
Fava Bean Stew

SERVES 4 AS A SIDE

1 pound (450 g) fava beans, fresh or frozen, shelled

5 tablespoons (75 ml) olive oil

1 small onion, cut crosswise and thinly sliced

2 garlic cloves, crushed

2 sprigs of fresh fennel tops (optional)

1 scant teaspoon salt

½ teaspoon pepper, or more to taste

½ cup (125 ml) Tomato Passata (page 237)

About ½ cup (125 ml) water or Vegetable Stock (page 32)

Bring a large pot of water to a boil over high heat and boil the fava beans for about 20 minutes. (If you are using frozen fava beans, this step is not necessary.) Heat the olive oil in a large pan over medium-high heat and add the onion and garlic. Sauté for 5 to 8 minutes, until translucent. Add the fava beans, fennel tops (if using), salt, pepper, tomato passata, and water. Reduce the heat to low and cook, half-covered, for 20 to 25 minutes, until the mixture has thickened. Remove and discard the garlic. You can serve as is or scoop up half of the fava beans, puree them in a blender, and stir them back in. Serve with toasted whole sourdough bread rubbed with garlic and brushed with extra-virgin olive oil.

IF MAKING WITH DRIED FAVA BEANS: If you want to make this with dried fava beans, use half the amount (½ lb [225 g]) and make sure you soak them for at least 18 hours and up to 24 hours in cold water. Drain the fava beans and proceed with the recipe. Cook the dried fava beans as you would the fresh, but add 1½ cups (375 ml) water instead of just ½ cup (125 ml) and simmer for 45 minutes, or until the fava beans are soft (it could take up to 1½ hours, depending on the fava beans).

FOR A GLUTEN-FREE VERSION: Serve with brown rice.

"ROMAGNA-STYLE" MEANS topping a dish with a bread crumb mixture flavored with parsley, garlic, pepper, and olive oil. Artichokes are especially good cooked this way, although they take a little prepping. In my family's tradition, these artichokes have always been part of our colorful Easter table, in addition to the Vegetable Graté with a Garlic-Herb Crumb Topping (page 213). They also make for a great Sunday side dish.

BRAISED ARTICHOKES
"Romagna-Style"

SERVES 6 AS A SIDE

For the crumb topping:

1 recipe Crumb Topping "Alla Romagnola" (page 49)

Large handful of pine nuts, finely chopped; a bunch of fresh basil (optional)

For the artichokes:

12 fresh Siena artichokes

½ lemon

2 tablespoons olive oil

¾ to 1 cup (175 ml to 250 ml) white wine

½ teaspoon salt

½ teaspoon pepper

1. **Make the crumb topping:** Follow the instructions on page 49. If the bread crumbs seem too dry, add a bit more oil. They should mostly stick together. Store it in the fridge if you are not using right away—you can also make this a day or two before.

2. **Clean the artichokes:** Remove the first two crowns of outer leaves and cut off the tips, so that you are left with no thorny parts. Stick your thumb in the center of the cut part and spread the petals open to make room for the filling.

3. Prepare a bowl of cold water, squeeze in the lemon juice, then add the already-squeezed ½ lemon as well. Put the artichokes in the acidulated water as you prepare them. Cut off the stalk, cut a 1-inch (2.5-cm) piece of the stalks from the part where it was attached to the artichoke, and peel them.

4. **To assemble:** Drain the artichokes and pat them dry with a kitchen towel. Add the olive oil to a large pan that can fit all of the artichokes tightly (you don't want them to fall over). Sprinkle salt and pepper on top of each artichoke, stuff them with the crumb topping, and line them in the pan. You might have leftovers or not, depending on how much stuffing you prefer. Throw in the trimmed stalks as well. Heat the pan over medium-low heat and cook the artichokes for about 3 minutes, until they start to sizzle (do not move the artichokes as they cook). Add enough water to cover them halfway and cook,

TIP: For an extra-crispy crumb topping, once the artichokes are done cooking on the stovetop, broil them for 5 minutes. Make sure you are using a pan that can go in the oven.

half-covered, for about 15 minutes. At this point, the water should be reduced by half. Add the wine and cook for 30 to 40 minutes more, until the artichokes are soft (cooking time will depend on their size). (They kind of cook like Chinese dumplings—they get crispy on the bottom and steamed on top.)

5. To test for doneness, pierce the artichokes gently with a fork: They are ready when the petals detach easily and the fork can pierce them with no resistance. Finish cooking, uncovered, for 5 minutes. If the artichokes seem not tender enough, add a little more water and cook longer, half-covered.

MUCH LIKE TIRAMISU: Pistachio & White Chocolate (page 137), panna cotta is a card up the sleeve of many Italians when they want to serve something impressively delicious for dessert. But I love it because it's easy to make a delicious vegan variation, too. Authentic panna cotta uses heavy cream (sometimes thinned down with some milk), but instead of dairy, I use coconut milk to achieve the same richness. For texture I also use agar-agar, a kind of algae that is a natural gelling agent, instead of classic gelatin, which is made out of bone marrow. The bitter chocolate topping perfectly pairs with the caramel-y flavor of the panna cotta, but a raspberry or strawberry topping—or nothing at all—would also work beautifully.

COCONUT CARAMEL PANNA COTTA

With Chocolate

MAKES FIVE ½-CUP (125-ML) SERVINGS

For the panna cotta:

½ cup plus 3 heaping tablespoons (130 g) packed dark brown sugar

1½ cups plus 1 tablespoon (400 ml) (one 13.5-fl. oz can) full-fat coconut milk, divided

½ cup (125 ml) heavy cream (or almond or regular milk for a lighter, and vegan, result)

1 whole vanilla bean, split and seeds scraped

1 teaspoon (3 g) agar-agar powder

½ cup (125 ml) water

For the chocolate topping:

2 ounces (50 g) bitter dark chocolate (choose 70% to 85% cocoa solids)

2 tablespoons coconut oil or flavorless vegetable oil, such as sunflower

1. **Make the panna cotta:** Place the brown sugar in a medium pot. Add ¼ cup (50 ml) of the coconut milk.

2. Heat the pot over medium heat and cook for about 5 minutes, until the sugar dissolves and turns into a dark brown syrup. Reduce the heat to medium-low and cook, stirring constantly, for 3 to 4 minutes. The sugar should have turned dense and syrupy. Add the rest of the coconut milk and the heavy cream and stir well.

3. Add the vanilla bean seeds and pod to the coconut milk. Bring the mixture to a very gentle simmer (do not let it come to a full boil). Simmer for about 2 minutes, stirring often, until the sugar is completely dissolved and the mixture is heated through.

4. Meanwhile, in another small pot, whisk the agar-agar with ¼ cup (50 ml) of the water to dissolve it (it is okay if it is lumpy and does not dissolve completely). Heat the agar-agar over low heat for about 1 minute, until it starts to bubble. Add the remaining ¼ cup (50 ml) water and boil the agar-agar for

recipe continues

NOTE: If making the chocolate topping with coconut oil, it will thicken and solidify as it cools. If you have leftovers and want to return it to a runny state, simply reheat it over a bain-marie. If making the topping with sunflower oil, the sauce will stay runny but the oil might separate from the chocolate. In this case, just stir well before using.

5 minutes (boiling the agar-agar is very important—it will get rid of its natural seaweed smell). Keep stirring so that it does not stick to the bottom. It will have thickened.

5. Add ½ cup (125 ml) of the hot coconut milk mixture to the agar-agar. Boil, whisking constantly, for 1 minute more, then pour everything back into the pot with the rest of the coconut milk mixture. Simmer for about 2 minutes, whisking constantly, until the mixture starts to thicken slightly. Remove and discard the vanilla pod and set aside coconut milk mixture.

6. Pour the panna cotta into five small pudding molds and let cool before transferring it to the fridge. Let the molds set for at least 2 hours or up to overnight.

7. Make the topping: Place the chocolate and the coconut oil in a medium bowl and put it over a pot of boiling water, making sure the bowl does not touch the water (you can also use a double boiler over low heat). Gently stir until the chocolate is fully melted.

8. To serve, unmold the panna cottas onto dessert plates. Drizzle some chocolate sauce on top of each and serve.

FOR A CAPPUCCINO PANNA COTTA VARIATION: Add one espresso shot to the coconut milk mixture and melt the chocolate with ¼ cup (50 ml) brewed espresso instead of the water.

FOR A STRAWBERRY TOPPING VARIATION: Cut up some fresh, plump, sweet strawberries and marinate them in plenty of lemon juice and a little brown sugar for 1 to 2 hours, then spoon over the panna cotta. The slight tartness of this topping goes well with the intense flavor of dark brown sugar.

CROSTATA IS PROBABLY THE DESSERT WE'VE BAKED MOST IN OUR HOUSEHOLD throughout the years. It's easy to make, requires ingredients that are always in the pantry, and, for us, it's always a great way to finish up a jar of homemade jam that's been sitting in my grandma's fridge for too long. A sort of Italian version of a tart, crostata differs from its French counterpart in that it is puffier and crumblier—that is why the recipe includes baking soda. It is usually filled with jam, but you can also use seasonal fruit. The crust is very versatile and so it's easy to swap in other delicious fillings like pears and chocolate, apples and fig jam, or any other jam or fruit you fancy.

ALMOND CROSTATA
With Ricotta & Jam Filling

....

MAKES ONE 10-INCH (25-CM) CROSTATA

....

For the crust:

½ cup (2.8 oz/80 g) whole-wheat flour (see Note)

½ cup plus 1 tablespoon (2.8 oz/80 g) rice flour

½ cup plus 3 tablespoons (2.5 oz/70 g) almond flour

3 tablespoons (1 oz/30 g) potato starch

½ cup (3.5 oz/100 g) packed dark brown sugar

1 teaspoon baking powder

½ teaspoon baking soda

3 tablespoons (1.4 oz/40 g) cold unsalted butter

1 large egg

1 teaspoon vanilla extract

Grated zest of 1 small lemon

Almond milk or nondairy milk, if needed

1. **Make the crust:** Combine the whole-wheat flour, rice flour, almond flour, potato starch, brown sugar, baking powder, baking soda, butter, egg, vanilla, and lemon zest in a food processor and process until the dough comes together. (You can also make the dough in a bowl and just knead it with your hands.) Scrape it out and knead it briefly to incorporate any flour that may not have been combined. If the dough is crumbly, add milk by the teaspoon until it comes together. The dough should feel wet but not really sticky. Let it rest for at least 30 minutes, or prepare it the night before and refrigerate.

2. When ready, press the dough evenly into a 10-inch (25 cm) tart pan and set aside in the fridge while you prepare the filling.

3. **Make the filling:** Combine the egg yolk, brown sugar, and vanilla in a medium bowl and beat the mixture in a stand mixer or with a handheld mixer for at least 5 minutes, or until the mixture is foamy and has tripled in size. Add half the ricotta and beat. Add the remaining ricotta once the first half is creamy and smooth.

ingredients and recipe continue

For the filling:

1 large egg, separated

¼ cup (1.7 oz/50 g) packed dark brown sugar or honey

1 teaspoon vanilla extract

1½ cups (10.5 oz/300 g) fresh ricotta cheese

1½ cups (375 ml) cherry jam, strawberry jam, or any other jam you love

A handful almond slivers, to garnish

4. In another clean, dry bowl, beat the egg white until stiff. Mix one-third of the egg whites into the ricotta mixture and, once fully incorporated, gently fold in the rest.

5. Preheat the oven to 350°F (180°C).

6. Take the crust out of the fridge and spread ½ cup (125 ml) of the jam on the bottom. Spread the ricotta mixture on top, then dollop on the rest of the jam and marble it with the spoon or spatula you are using. Sprinkle with almond slivers and bake for 35 to 45 minutes, until the ricotta is set and the crust is golden (cooking time depends on your oven).

7. When the crostata is ready, the crust will feel soft to the touch and it might seem undercooked, but if it has browned on top it is done. If you leave it in the oven too long, it might turn a little tough. Test it with a toothpick and, if the toothpick comes out dry, it is ready. Turn off the oven and let it set for 5 minutes more before removing.

8. Wait for it to cool before unmolding and slicing, as crostata is very crumbly when hot.

NOTE: You can substitute the whole-wheat flour with fine polenta meal to make a gluten-free version.

VARIATIONS: Instead of jam, you can marble the ricotta with the pistachio butter from the Tiramisu recipe (see Tiramisu: Pistachio & White Chocolate, page 137) or chocolate hazelnut butter, or mix either of those with Classic Vanilla Custard (page 51) before baking.

FOR ITALIANS, THE TERM *TORTA DELLA NONNA* refers not only to the classic cake with custard and pine nuts (see Torta Della Nonna with Lemon Custard, page 224) but also to any earthy, homey baked pie, tart, or cake that brings to mind the sweet smells that constantly seemed to permeate the kitchens of our grandmas. *Nonnas* hardly ever use fancy spices, but they load their cakes with lemon zest and seasonal fruit. Prune coffee cake is a traditional recipe in Romagna, and here is my vegan take—no eggs, butter, or lard involved.

MY NONNA'S PRUNE CAKE
With Dried Fruit

....

MAKES ONE 10-INCH (25 CM) CAKE

....

¼ cup (50 ml) organic sunflower oil or vegetable oil, plus more for greasing the pan

1 cup (7 oz/200 g) packed light brown sugar, plus 1 teaspoon for the pan

1 cup (5.3 oz/150 g) whole-wheat flour

1 cup (4.6 oz/130 g) white spelt flour (see Note)

⅓ cup (1.7 oz/50 g) potato starch

1 heaping teaspoon baking soda

1 heaping teaspoon baking powder

Grated zest and juice of 1 lemon

1 teaspoon ground cinnamon (optional)

1¾ cups (375 ml) almond milk or soy milk

1 tablespoon apple cider vinegar

¼ cup (50 ml) water

2 teaspoons vanilla extract

Pinch of salt

15 medium prunes or plums, halved and pitted

⅓ cup (1.7 oz/50 g) dried fruit, such as raisins or apricots

1. Preheat the oven to 350°F (180°C). Line a 10-inch (25 cm) springform pan with parchment paper and lightly oil the sides. Sprinkle about a teaspoon of brown sugar on the bottom.

2. Combine the whole-wheat flour, white spelt flour, potato starch, baking soda, baking powder, brown sugar, and lemon zest in a large bowl and whisk to break any lumps. If using cinnamon, add it at this point.

3. In a large glass measuring cup, combine the almond milk, vinegar, and lemon juice and stir. After a few seconds, the milk will start to curdle. Immediately add the water, sunflower oil, and vanilla. Stir well. Slowly pour this into the dry mix, stirring with a whisk to break any lumps. The batter will be somewhat on the liquid side.

4. Cut each plum into ¼-inch (5 mm) wedges and arrange in a circle in the prepared springform pan, until the bottom is completely filled. Sprinkle the dried fruit on top, and slowly pour the cake batter in. Bake for 40 to 50 minutes, until cooked through. Test the center of the cake with a toothpick to make sure it is cooked through. Once cooked and golden on top, turn off the oven and let it sit in the oven for 5 minutes more.

5. Remove the cake from oven and let cool. Serve with a simple dusting of powdered sugar, almond slivers, or a dollop of yogurt.

NOTE: I like using stone-milled white spelt flour in this recipe. See if you can find it.

FOR A FALL FRUIT VARIATION: Use pears instead of plums, ⅓ cup (1.7 oz/50 g) chopped hazelnuts instead of the dried fruit, and ⅓ cup chocolate chips. Sprinkle the walnuts and chocolate chips over the pears before pouring in the batter.

FOR A WINTER FRUIT VARIATION: Use apples instead of plums, ⅓ cup (1.7 oz/50 g) raisins for the dried fruit, add ⅓ cup (1.7 oz/50 g) chopped walnuts. Flavor the batter with 1 to 2 teaspoons cinnamon and a pinch of nutmeg.

VISCIOLE IS A VARIETY OF CHERRY indigenous to the Le Marche region. When spring markets start, farmers pull out basketfuls of this kind of pleasantly sour cherry, and they usually sell out within the first half of the morning. They are widely used in sweet and savory preparations alike and their intense taste produces a sweet wine that is to die for. I find that their cherry flavor goes great with the bitter Sicilian almonds used for amaretti, and this gluten-free cake is the perfect proof that these two ingredients can marry joyfully. If you cannot find visciole, just use the ripest, juiciest cherries you can get your hands on at the market.

ALMOND AMARETTO CAKE
With Visciole Cherries

MAKES ONE 9-INCH (22 CM) CAKE

For the cherries:

2 pounds (900 g) cherries, pitted and halved

Juice of ½ lemon

1 heaping tablespoon packed brown sugar

1 to 2 tablespoons rum or maraschino

For the cake batter:

⅓ cup (75 ml) coconut oil, plus more for greasing the pan

½ cup (2.6 oz/75 g) whole spelt flour

⅓ cup (1.4 oz/40 g) white spelt flour

½ cup (3.5 oz/100 g) packed light brown sugar

2 teaspoons baking soda

Pinch of salt

1 cup (4.9 oz/70 g) almonds

3 large eggs

2 teaspoons vanilla extract

½ scant teaspoon amaretto flavoring or almond extract

⅓ cup (75 ml) plant or regular milk

Slivered almonds, to sprinkle on top

1. **Prepare the cherries:** Place the cherries, lemon juice, brown sugar, and rum in a medium-large pan. Cook over medium-low heat for about 5 minutes, until the lemon, brown sugar, and rum form a syrup and the cherries are soft. Set aside.

2. Preheat the oven to 350°F (180°C). Line a 9-inch (22-cm) springform pan with parchment paper and grease the sides.

3. **Make the cake batter:** Combine the whole spelt flour, white spelt flour, ¼ cup (1.7 oz/50 g) of the brown sugar, the baking soda, and the salt and whisk to combine. Grind the almonds in a coffee grinder, blitzing a few seconds at a time, until you have a fine meal. Add the ground almonds to the dry ingredients.

4. Separate the eggs. Add the vanilla and amaretto to the yolks and cream them with the remaining ¼ cup (1.7 oz/50 g) packed brown sugar. Once fluffy, add the coconut oil and milk. Gradually whisk in the flour mixture. Beat the egg whites until stiff, then fold them into the batter until fully incorporated. Scrape the cherries into the batter and fold them in as well.

5. Pour in the batter into the prepared pan. Sprinkle with almond slivers and bake for 30 to 40 minutes, depending on your oven. Check for doneness with a toothpick: If it comes out clean when inserted into the middle of the cake, the cake is ready.

6. Serve as is with tea or coffee, or with yogurt or ice cream.

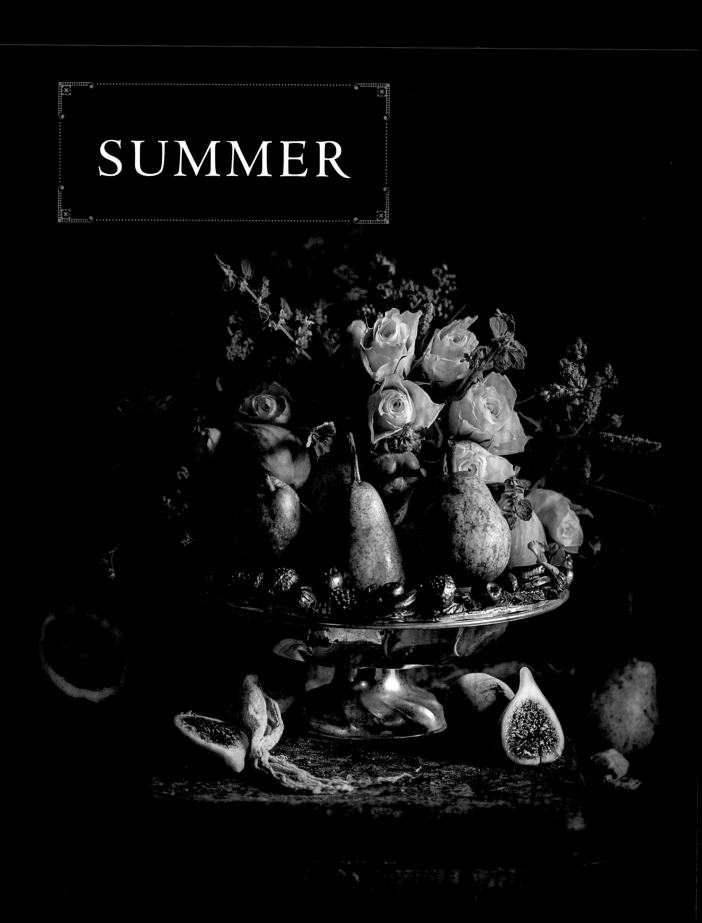

SUMMER

Each year as the warm weather starts to heat the ocher walls of our family home, a funny thing occurs: Cars of lost tourists, looking for their way to Gradara, stop at our place and ask with lit-up eyes whether it is the agriturismo, or bed-and-breakfast, they are looking for. Their mistake is understandable: Our house is close to the castle, and the surrounding area is full of country houses with rooms for tourists. The confused visitors approach once a day on average—proof that our countryside is sure a sight to be seen.

Gradara also has the advantage of being just five minutes from the seaside. But, beautiful as the local beaches are, the sight I love the most in the summer are the golden wheat, barley, and farro fields that set the landscape ablaze with gold.

"When I was young, wheat strands seemed to be so tall," my mom says every year. "We would spend hours running in the wheat fields, getting lost among the poppy flowers and golden strands."

And, though the wheat may have changed, some things never change in this beautiful season: the song of the crickets, making an orchestral din in the heat of midday. The bushes of four-o'clocks blooming after sunset. Gelato dripping down our fingers as we race to lick it faster than it melts, or granita sipped with a thick straw. Picking and eating fruit fresh from the trees, carrying our baskets up the ladder: the last cherries first, then apricots, then peaches, then plums, and finally figs. Making large vats of jam with the plentiful harvest, the sticky jars cooling upside down on tea towels, and the kitchen spotted with stains of strawberry or peach jam. The long bike rides, the picnics, and the sunburns. Cooking outdoors together, and the fresh produce from our garden—especially the unbelievable flood of zucchini. This, and much more, makes up our summer in the countryside year after year.

This, of course, and all the lost tourists on their way to the castle.

Maybe one day, we will indeed turn this place into a bed-and-breakfast, one where people could experience life with nature, animals, and great local food.

But that's a dream for another time.

RECIPES

Mains

Couscous & Chickpea Croquettes with Eggplant & Olives

Pan-Sautéed Pasta with Garlicky Cherry Tomatoes

Ricotta Gnocchi with Saffron, Zucchini & Cherry Tomatoes

Piadina Romagnola with Grilled Vegetables & Tomato Pesto

Stuffed Tomatoes with Millet & Rice Stuffing

Vegetable Parmigiana with a Hint of Scamorza

Emilia-Style Vegetable Burgers

Summer Panino with Marinated Eggplant, Mozzarella & Pesto

Sides & Salads

Millet & Rice Stuffing for Vegetables

August Salad with Lentils, Barley & Mediterranean Flavors

Vegetable Graté with a Garlic-Herb Crumb Topping

Grilled Vegetables with a Garlic & Parsley Dressing

"Il Pastrocchio," Summer Mixed Vegetable Tray

Sweets & Desserts

Wine-Poached Peaches with Almond Cream

Coffee Bavarese, a No-Bake "Cheesecake"

"Bewitched" Ricotta Mousse with Roasted Balsamic Grapes

Torta Della Nonna with Lemon Custard

TIP: You can also bake the croquettes. Line a rimmed baking sheet with oiled parchment paper and bake them in a 425°F (220°C) oven until crispy.

IT IS FUNNY how the best recipes are sometimes born out of a casualty: These croquettes were actually the result of a failed attempt to make stuffing for another recipe. I tossed some leftover ingredients together, and what I ended up with was a doughy, intensely flavorful mixture that smelled like the perfumes of the Mediterranean and the shores of Sicily and the Far East. I decided to assemble croquettes out of my impromptu mixture, inspired by the tiny meatballs commonly served at *aperitivos* (the Italian happy hour). These croquettes definitely smell like summer, but they are perfectly doable year-round.

COUSCOUS & CHICKPEA CROQUETTES
With Eggplant & Olives

MAKES ABOUT 25 CROQUETTES

½ cup (2.8 oz/80 g) whole-wheat couscous

2 tablespoons olive oil, plus more for brushing the eggplant if softening in the oven

2 small eggplants, diced

1 cup (5.6 oz/160 g) cooked chickpeas

1 tablespoon fine whole-wheat or rye bread crumbs, plus more for coating

¼ cup (a large handful) tightly packed basil and parsley, finely chopped

Oregano

1 tablespoon capers, soaked, squeezed out, and finely chopped

½ cup (2 oz/ 50 g) pitted olives of your choice, chopped

2 tablespoons tomato paste

¼ cup (50 ml) sun-dried tomatoes preserved in olive oil, finely chopped

1 scant teaspoon salt

1. Heat 1 tablespoon of the olive oil in a medium pan over medium heat and add the eggplants. Sauté for 1 minute, then add 2 tablespoons water, cover, and cook for about 15 minutes, until the eggplant is soft and the water has evaporated. (Alternatively, preheat the oven to 400°F [205°C]. Cut the eggplants in half, lightly brush with olive oil, and bake for 20 to 25 minutes, or until soft. Then scoop out the flesh.)

2. Mash the chickpeas with a fork in a large bowl. Add the cooked eggplants, couscous, bread crumbs, basil-parsley mix, oregano, capers, olives, tomato paste, sun-dried tomatoes, and salt. Mix well with your hands to combine.

3. Spread the bread crumbs on a baking sheet or large plate. With slightly oiled or wet hands, form little balls with the eggplant-chickpea mixture and delicately toss each ball in the bread crumbs to coat them well.

4. Heat the remaining 1 tablespoon olive oil in a medium pan over medium heat. Once hot, cook the croquettes for about 2 minutes, until well browned. Flip and brown the other side as well. Cook in batches if necessary, and add more oil if needed (see Tip).

5. Serve with Pesto Ligure (page 40) and some green salad.

ONE OF THE FIRST DISHES every Italian kid eats is pasta al pomodoro, pasta with tomato sauce. Most of the year we enjoy pasta al pomodoro with tomato passata, but when the summer garden is speckled with jewel-like tomatoes of every form and shape, we use the ripest, juiciest cherry tomatoes the garden can produce instead. This dish is likely one of the simplest, quickest recipes in this book, yet for me and anyone else who grew up with it, it is also one of the tastiest. It smells intensely of basil and garlic, and every bite brings fond memories of the scorching sun in the countryside, the crickets singing, bike rides in the dusty road, and the hot tomato juice dripping down my chin.

PAN-SAUTÉED PASTA
With Garlicky Cherry Tomatoes

SERVES 3 OR 4

Coarse salt, for the pasta water

½ cup (120 ml) extra-virgin olive oil

6 large garlic cloves, sliced

Pinch of dried red pepper flakes

1½ pounds (675 g) cherry tomatoes, halved

1 teaspoon salt

Pepper (about a pinch)

About ½ cup (125 ml) chopped olives (optional)

10 fresh basil leaves

10 ounces (310 g) whole-wheat or spelt pasta of your choice

1. Bring a large pot of water to a rolling boil over high heat, adding salt in the proportion of 1 scant teaspoon for every 4 cups (1 l) water.

2. Heat the olive oil in a medium-large pan over medium-low heat. Test the temperature by dropping in a garlic slice. The oil is hot enough if the garlic sizzles slightly. Add the rest of the garlic. Cook, stirring, for about 1 minute, then add the red pepper flakes, cherry tomatoes, salt, and black pepper. Add the olives, if using. Cook, stirring, for about 15 minutes, until the tomatoes release their water and turn soft, creating a sauce with the oil. Tear the basil leaves into pieces and add to the tomato sauce.

3. Cook the pasta according to the package instructions and, when there are about 4 minutes of cooking time left, drain the pasta, saving ⅓ cup (75 ml) of the pasta water, and add the pasta straight into the pan with the sauce (it is okay if some of the pasta water drips in). Reduce the heat to medium and add about 3 tablespoons of the reserved pasta water. Toss the pasta to coat with the sauce, letting the starch from the pasta water mingle with the sauce and turn creamy. Cook for 2 minutes and add the remaining 2 tablespoons pasta water. Cook for 2 minutes more. When the pasta is cooked and the water is absorbed into the sauce, remove the pasta from the heat. Serve immediately.

I LOVE STUFFING MY VEGETABLES with delicious savory fillings, especially in the summer when tomatoes—which are perfect for stuffing—are plentiful. Every Mediterranean country has its own tradition of stuffed tomatoes, and the Italian recipe is similar to the Greek *gemista* preparation. I prefer to keep my dairy intake low so I don't always add the mozzarella, but it sure makes for a tasty addition along with the bold Mediterranean summer flavors in the recipe. Eat these and transport yourself to a pretty village by the sea, with seagulls calling and a gentle wind caressing your bare legs.

STUFFED TOMATOES
With Millet & Rice Stuffing

SERVES 6 AS AN APPETIZER, 2 AS A MAIN

6 ripe medium red-vine tomatoes, weighing about 3 pounds (1.3 kg)

3 or 4 pinches of salt

½ recipe for Millet & Rice Stuffing for Vegetables (page 209)

½ recipe for Tomato Sauce (page 33)

½ mozzarella ball, cut into small cubes (optional)

Olive oil, for brushing

2 tablespoons grated Grana or pecorino cheese

1. Preheat the oven to 475°F (245°C).

2. Cut off the top part of the tomatoes, scoop out the seeds, and sprinkle a little salt inside each. Arrange them on a griddle, cut-side down, and cook them over medium heat for 10 minutes.

3. Mix the tomato sauce and the mozzarella cubes with the stuffing.

4. Brush a small rimmed baking dish (about 11 × 7 inches/ 28 × 18 cm) or casserole with olive oil and arrange the tomatoes cut-side up. Stuff each tomato with the stuffing, so that it slightly heaps out, and sprinkle the grated cheese on each tomato. Lightly drizzle with oil.

5. Reduce the oven temperature to 450°F (230°C) and bake for 15 to 20 minutes, until the cheese is melted and the top is slightly browned. Serve warm, or enjoy cold the next day.

EGGPLANT PARMIGIANA IS one of the most indulgent, most delicious Italian summer dishes, when the sun-bathed gardens fill with those dark purple, magical vegetables. In the classic recipe, the eggplants are fried, then layered with lots of cheese. Some people get fancier with additions like sliced hard-boiled eggs, or they'll even use Bolognese for the stuffing. I prefer to keep the dish much lighter, especially when the weather is hot. In my recipe, the eggplants are baked or grilled and layered with zucchini, and you can really use as much cheese as you like—even just a tiny bit makes this dish taste delicious.

VEGETABLE PARMIGIANA
With a Hint of Scamorza

SERVES 4 TO 6; MAKES A 12 × 8-INCH (30 × 20-CM) CASSEROLE

1½ pounds (about 700 g) round eggplants (about 2 medium)

Plenty of salt for sweating the eggplants

1½ pounds (about 700 g) zucchini (about 4 medium)

1 recipe Tomato Sauce (page 33)

¾ cup (80 g) grated Grana or pecorino cheese

About ½ pound (450 g) Scamorza cheese (or even less if you want to keep it light), thinly sliced

Olive oil, for brushing

1. Slice the eggplants lengthwise to slightly thicker than ¼ inch. Lay the slices in a single layer in a colander, sprinkle evenly with salt, then repeat until you run out of slices. Set aside for at least 1 hour to sweat out their bitter liquid.

2. Slice the zucchini lengthwise into slightly thinner slices.

3. Rinse the eggplant briefly and pat dry.

4. Preheat the oven to 400°F (205°C). Prepare a rimmed baking sheet and brush it well with olive oil, then arrange the eggplant and zucchini slices without overlapping and brush again with olive oil. Bake for 25 to 30 minutes, until tender and cooked through.

5. Prepare a 12 × 8-inch (30 × 20-cm) casserole and cover the bottom with 3 tablespoons of the tomato sauce. Layer the vegetables, alternating eggplants and zucchini so that they completely cover the bottom—it is okay if they overlap a bit. Cover with a third of the tomato sauce, then cover with thin Scamorza slices, and finish with a third of the grated cheese. Repeat to make three layers.

6. Bake for 30 to 40 minutes, until the top is nice and golden. Let cool for 10 minutes before slicing and serving. This dish is also great served reheated.

ALTHOUGH THINGS ARE RAPIDLY CHANGING, Emilia, the northernmost part of the Emilia-Romagna region, has not been known as a vegetarian-friendly place. I have heard many stories of American tourists being shocked at how often they saw whole prosciuttos hanging off the shop windows, and Bologna, Modena, and Reggio Emilia are famous for still using lard most often as a cooking fat. But Emilia is also famous for its incredible balsamic vinegar and its seasoned cheeses, which are easy to find made with vegetarian rennet. This luscious veggie burger is inspired by my favorite meatless Emilian flavors.

EMILIA-STYLE VEGETABLE BURGERS

MAKES 4 BURGERS

For the burgers:

1 tablespoon olive oil, plus more for brushing

1 large onion, finely chopped

2 medium shallots, finely chopped

2 slices whole-wheat bread (total weight 2 oz/60 g)

½ cup (125 ml) regular or nondairy milk

3 garlic cloves

3 cups (17 oz/480 g) cooked chickpeas

¼ cup (1 oz/30 g) chopped walnuts

½ cup (125 ml) parsley, finely chopped

½ cup (125 ml) packed basil

1 small sprig of fresh rosemary, chopped (1 tablespoon chopped)

¼ cup (1 oz/30 g) grated hard cheese such as pecorino or Grana cheese (substitute nutritional yeast if vegan)

2 tablespoons ground flaxseeds in 4 tablespoons (50 ml) water, or 1 egg

½ teaspoon salt

½ teaspoon ground coriander

Pepper

To assemble:

4 whole-wheat burger buns

Grilled Vegetables with a Garlic & Parsley Dressing (page 215) and/or fresh arugula

Stracchino cheese, or thin Grana shavings (skip if vegan)

Vegan mayo

1. Make the burgers: Heat the olive oil in a large pan over medium-low heat. Add the onion and shallots and sauté for about 20 minutes, stirring often, until they turn golden. If they stick to the bottom of the pan, add a splash of water.

2. Place the bread, milk, garlic, chickpeas, walnuts, parsley, basil, rosemary, cheese, flaxseeds, salt, coriander, and pepper in a food processor and process until a dough forms. Scrape the dough out and divide it into four parts. Shape each part into a patty.

3. Preheat the oven to 400°F (205°C).

4. Oil a rimmed baking sheet and arrange the burgers on it. Generously brush each burger with olive oil. Bake for 15 minutes, until slightly browned. You can also cook them in an oiled griddle or skillet.

5. To assemble the burgers: Toast the burger buns on a griddle and layer the patties, grilled vegetables, cheese, caramelized onions, and mayo if desired.

I HAVE ALWAYS FOUND IT CURIOUS how the word *panino* in the United States refers to a sort of sub sandwich pressed with a hot griddle or panini press. In Italy, the word *panino* is any kind of sandwich made with Italian crusty bread, and to me and many others, it brings back memories of school trips, lunches—and quite often breakfasts, as we stopped in little bottegas along the way to buy them to order—made with freshly baked bread. This panino in particular is one my friends and I would sometime stop and buy before school at a small Sardinian shop. We'd nibble on it during class, making sure we remained unseen.

SUMMER PANINO
With Marinated Eggplant, Mozzarella & Pesto

MAKES 1 PANINO

For the Marinated Eggplants:

2 medium-long eggplants

1 teaspoon salt

½ cup (125 ml) extra-virgin olive oil

1 small garlic clove, finely sliced

1 small bunch of parsley (about 15 sprigs), finely minced

1 handful of basil leaves (about 15), finely minced

1 tablespoon lemon juice

2 to 3 tablespoons balsamic vinegar

2 slices whole rye sourdough bread, or your favorite whole sourdough bread, or some ciabatta bread

Pesto Ligure (page 40)

Tomato slices

Fresh buffalo mozzarella

Grilled Marinated Eggplant

Extra toppings: Zucchini in Olive Oil (page 235); arugula or other greens

1. **Make the eggplants:** Cut each eggplant into ⅛-inch-thick (3-mm) strips, preferably with the help of a mandoline slicer. Toss the slices in a bowl with the salt.

2. Heat a griddle or cast-iron skillet over medium-high heat (if you do not have either, use a nonstick pan). Grill the eggplants until soft, about 40 seconds per side. (It will take up to 2 minutes per side if using a nonstick pan, or if the slices are thicker than ⅛ inch.)

3. Toss the eggplant in bowl with the remaining ingredients. Lay the eggplant slices in a resealable plastic container and store in the fridge for a couple hours before using. If you do not want to use raw garlic, omit it and use half extra virgin olive oil and half garlic oil (page 245).

4. Slather the slices of bread with the basil sauce. Layer one slice of bread with tomato, mozzarella, and marinated eggplants, and cover with the other slice. You can either eat this as is or finish it in a panini press if you so desire! Serve it with a simple green salad for a wonderful quick lunch.

NOTE: It's best to assemble the sandwich when you are ready to eat it. To pack it up, drain the eggplant from the oil well, then tightly wrap it in plastic wrap separately from the bread and the other fillings.

THIS MAKES A NICE, naturally gluten-free, multipurpose stuffing for all kinds of vegetables, but it is also delicious as a salad served on its own. I love to pair it with Grilled Vegetables with a Garlic & Parsley Dressing (page 215), or I'll toss in some fresh or cooked vegetables if I am having it as a main dish. It is a great side year-round, but I enjoy it the most when it's fresh and cool out of the fridge on a warm summer evening.

MILLET & RICE STUFFING
For Vegetables

SERVES 2

½ cup (3.5 oz/100 g) millet

½ cup (3.5 oz/100 g) brown rice

¼ cup (3.5 oz/100 g) fresh parsley

¼ cup (a full cupped hand) packed fresh basil leaves, finely chopped

2 tablespoons finely chopped fresh mint

A few sprigs of fresh fennel, finely chopped

⅓ cup (1.7 oz/50 g) toasted hazelnuts, coarsely chopped

⅓ cup (1.7 oz/50 g) nuts of your choice, toasted and coarsely chopped

1 scant teaspoon salt

1 tablespoon lemon juice

3 tablespoons extra-virgin olive oil, preferably garlic infused (see page 245)

Optional add ins:

1 ball fresh mozzarella cheese, chopped

A handful arugula, chopped

Any vegetable preserved in olive oil, chopped

1. Cook the millet and rice in separate pots, as they have different cooking times. Check the packages for cooking instructions.

2. Toss the cooked millet and rice in a large bowl with the parsley, basil, mint, fennel, hazelnuts, toasted nuts, salt, lemon juice, olive oil, and mozzarella or other add-ins, if using, and adjust the seasoning to taste. If you keep it in the fridge overnight, it will get even more tasty.

3. Use the mixture for Stuffed Tomatoes with Millet & Rice Stuffing (page 202) or Stuffed Artichokes with Peas (page 165). It is also great for stuffing raw, halved peppers for a light meal.

PLUMP, BRIGHT RED TOMATOES speckle every inch of our vegetable garden starting in late June, but it is in early August that they seem to burst with color and flavor, hanging like shimmering jewels off their vines. Around the same time, we harvest Tropea onions, the famed sweet red onions named after a town in Calabria. To make this colorful salad, we also collect some arugula, basil, and marjoram. It is one of our favorite summer lunches.

AUGUST SALAD
With Lentils, Barley & Mediterranean Flavors

SERVES 4

For the dressing:

¼ cup (a full cupped hand) packed fresh basil

1 sprig of fresh marjoram

Juice of ½ lemon

3 tablespoons extra-virgin olive oil, plus more to drizzle

1 teaspoon salt, or more or less to taste

For the salad:

1 cup (7 oz/200 g) lentils

1 cup (7 oz/200 g) whole barley, soaked overnight

2 cups (2.1 oz/60 g) packed arugula

1 pound (450 g) cherry tomatoes, halved

1 medium red Tropea onion

2 tablespoons capers, soaked, rinsed, and finely chopped

⅓ cup (1.7 oz/50 g) pine nuts, lightly toasted

Extras: mozzarella bocconcini, Marinated Olives (page 232)

1. Make the dressing: Place the basil, marjoram, lemon juice, olive oil, and salt in a food processor and process. (Or chop the basil as finely as you can, add it to a jar with all of the other ingredients, and shake well to combine.)

2. Make the salad: Boil the lentils and barley separately, until cooked. The lentils should take 20 to 30 minutes, while the whole barley should take around 45 minutes. Drain well and set aside until cool.

3. Chop some of the arugula and leave some whole. Quarter some of the tomatoes (use colorful heirloom tomatoes for a prettier effect). Place the lentils, barley, arugula, cherry tomatoes, onion, capers, and pine nuts in a serving bowl, pour the dressing on, and toss to combine. To enjoy it at its best, let it cool in the fridge for about 1 hour. You can also use this salad to make Stuffed Tomatoes with Millet & Rice Stuffing (page 202).

IF THERE IS A SIDE THAT IS NEVER—and I mean never—missing from my family's holiday table, it is vegetable *graté*. Whether it's Christmas, New Year's, Easter, birthdays, or any other gathering, vegetable gratin is there. Sometimes, we even use out-of-season vegetables to make it. It's a quintessential recipe that all nonnas from Romagna have up their sleeve for every season, and it makes a deliciously summery stuffing for piadinas (see page 199) cooked over the fired-up griddles on the Riviera Romagnola and served at hot summer festivals at the beach.

VEGETABLE GRATÉ
With a Garlic-Herb Crumb Topping

SERVES 4 TO 6

Crumb Topping "Alla Romagnola" (page 49)

3 small long eggplants

Salt

2 medium white or yellow onions

2 red or yellow bell peppers

3 medium ripe Roma tomatoes, or other round and plump varieties

Olive oil, for drizzling

1. Make the crumb topping per the instructions on page 49.

2. Preheat the oven to 425°F (220°C).

3. Cut the eggplants in half and make several cross incisions along the cut side. Sprinkle with salt and let stand in a colander for 20 minutes. When ready, pat the tops dry with a paper towel.

4. Steam the onions in a steamer basket placed in a pot over 1 inch (2.5 cm) of simmering water (or use your favorite steaming method) for about 10 minutes, until softened. Then cut the onions in half.

5. Cut the bell peppers in half and scoop out all of the seeds.

6. Cut the tomatoes in half and scoop out the seeds. Lightly sprinkle them with salt. Arrange them cut-side down on the oven rack with a rimmed baking sheet below to collect the juices, and bake for 10 minutes. Do not turn off the oven, as you are about to bake all of the vegetables.

7. Arrange the tomatoes, onions, and bell peppers cut-side up on a well-oiled rimmed baking sheet. Add the eggplant, cut-side up, to a separate baking dish. Distribute the bread mixture

recipe continues

TIP: The graté freezes very well. Just arrange the vegetables into freezer trays (stacking them one on top of the other is fine) and defrost. Finish them under the broiler for 5 minutes.

evenly to top all of the vegetables, then drizzle a little bit of olive oil. In the eggplant baking dish, pour about ¼ inch (5 cm) water and loosely cover with aluminum foil. Bake all of the vegetables for 20 to 25 minutes. When the water is completely absorbed, remove the aluminum foil from both baking sheets and broil for 5 minutes, until the topping crisps up. Serve as an accompaniment to Piadina Romagnola with Grilled Vegetables & Tomato Pesto (page 199) or any other dish—it goes wonderfully with everything.

FOR A WINTER VARIATION: You can use the same crumb topping with fennel (slice into wedges or thick slices and lightly steam before baking), squash (slice into half-moons and bake), mushrooms (stuff the caps and bake), and cauliflower (break into florets and steam or blanch for 5 minutes before tossing with the crumb mixture and baking).

"MARISA IS GOING TO BRING HER GRILLED VEGETABLES, YES?" is what everyone would say when they knew my mom was coming to a dinner party. No other woman can make any sentient being fall in love with vegetables like my mom can. Clearly, I learned from the best. When we have so much zucchini in our summer garden that we don't know what to do with it anymore, this recipe is a perfect, tasty choice (along with the Zucchini in Olive Oil, page 235). Serve these grilled vegetables with any dish, as a sandwich filling or pizza topping, or just on their own on a slice of homemade sourdough bread.

GRILLED VEGETABLES
With a Garlic & Parsley Dressing

SERVES 4

For the dressing:

3 tablespoons balsamic vinegar

¼ cup (a full cupped hand) packed fresh parsley, finely chopped

10 fresh basil leaves, finely sliced

⅓ cup (75 ml) extra-virgin olive oil

1 teaspoon salt

2 or 3 mint leaves (optional)

For the vegetables:

2 large eggplants, any kind

4 medium zucchini

1. Make the dressing: Combine the vinegar, parsley, basil, olive oil, salt, and mint leaves, if using, in a jar and shake.

2. Make the vegetables: Heat a griddle or nonstick pan over high heat. Slice the eggplants and zucchini thinly, about ⅛ inch (3 mm) or even thinner if you can manage it (it is best to use a mandoline). Grill in batches, about 1 minute per side, or until the zucchini is soft and has grill marks. After they are cooked, transfer them to a baking sheet or bowl. Once done, add the dressing and mix well—use your hands to coat every slice evenly. Chill for at least 1 hour. They are even better prepared a day in advance and left to marinate for a bit.

NOTE: In the winter, try this dressing on boiled brassicas, beets, or any roasted vegetable. This dressing really works with any cooked vegetable—just remember to let them marinate before serving!

EVERY SUMMER, around the beginning of July, my grandpa drops boxes full of summer vegetables from our garden in front of our door, and each time we are presented the same question: "So, what shall you do with these?" We run our hands through our hair as we think of the answer. Aside from Vegetable Graté with a Garlic-Herb Crumb Topping (page 213), what can we cook? Pastrocchio, of course.

Pastrocchio means "mess" in Italian, the kind of mess you would make if you decided to paint a wall various colors using your hands. The word surely recalls the pretty mix of colors in this dish. I love this recipe so much that, over time, I have learned to anticipate my grandpa and pick the vegetables before he does.

"I don't know what's with the garden," he grunts. "Doesn't produce as much as it used to."

"IL PASTROCCHIO"
Summer Mixed Vegetable Tray

SERVES 4

2 large onions

1 pound (450 g) cherry tomatoes

2 medium eggplants, round or long

2 medium zucchini

1 large red or yellow bell pepper

1 large green bell pepper

3 tablespoons olive oil, plus more for oiling the baking dish

1 teaspoon salt

Basil, marjoram, thyme, or herbs of choice

Pepper

1. Quarter the onions and slice them lengthwise quite thin. Halve the cherry tomatoes and cut the eggplants and zucchini into ¼-inch (5-mm) cubes. Discard the seeds from the bell peppers, cut them into quarters, then cut them crosswise into pieces.

2. Preheat the oven to 400°F (205°C). Lightly oil a baking dish that can fit all of the vegetables.

3. Heat a nonstick pan over high heat. Place the onions in a bowl and toss with 1 tablespoon of the olive oil. When the pan is hot, pour in the onions and cook, stirring, for about 15 minutes, until softened and golden. Transfer to the baking dish.

4. Add the zucchini and eggplant to the same bowl, and toss with 1 tablespoon of the olive oil. Add to the pan and sauté for 8 to 10 minutes. Transfer to the dish with the onions. Add the peppers and tomatoes to the bowl, toss with the last 1 tablespoon olive oil, and add to the pan. Sauté for about 8 minutes, until slightly browned. Transfer to the baking dish.

5. Sprinkle the salt over the vegetables, along with the herbs and pepper. Toss to coat evenly, and bake for about 20 minutes, or until the vegetables are soft.

6. Serve as a side to any summer dish.

IT IS NOT UNCOMMON DURING SUMMER FESTIVALS to see people holding glasses of cold wine with peaches dunked into them. For me, this summertime treat reminds me of my grandfather. I can see him in his tank top slicing peaches on our bread crumb–filled tablecloth after an outdoor meal. We'd let the peaches steep in white wine for a few minutes before impatiently diving in.

"We did not have any dessert," says my grandfather in his strong Romagna accent. He is now approaching ninety and he still slices peaches for everyone in his tank top after our summer meals. "You can keep all your fancy cakes. In the summer, it's *pesche col vino.*"

This recipe is inspired by that summer delight.

WINE-POACHED PEACHES
With Almond Cream

....

SERVES 3 TO 6

....

For the peaches:

3 medium peaches, halved, pits removed

1 cup (250 ml) white wine

1 cup (250 ml) freshly squeezed orange juice

1 tablespoon rum

2 tablespoons brown muscovado sugar

½ vanilla bean, seeds scraped

1 star anise

One 1-inch (2.5 cm) piece of cinnamon stick

For the cream:

Classic Vanilla Custard (page 51)

½ cup (125 ml) canned coconut milk, left to sit overnight in the fridge, or heavy cream

1 teaspoon almond extract

Toasted almonds and crumbled amaretti cookies (skip if vegan), for garnish

1. **Make the peaches:** Place the peaches in a shallow saucepan along with the wine, orange juice, rum, sugar, vanilla bean pod and seeds, star anise, and cinnamon stick. Cook over medium-low heat, covered, for about 5 minutes, until the peaches are soft. Remove the lid and cook for 5 minutes more. Remove the peaches with a slotted spoon and set aside on a plate.

2. Raise the heat to medium and let the syrup in the saucepan reduce by half. Let cool while you make the cream.

3. If you are using coconut cream, scoop the upper layer of coconut fat from the coconut milk can and whip it with the almond extract. If you are using heavy cream, whip it with the almond extract until almost stiff.

4. Fold the whipped cream into the almond custard, mixing gently until well combined.

5. Serve the peaches with a drizzle of syrup, the almond cream, and toasted almonds.

NOTE: You can also serve this with Lemon Custard (see page 51), or with coconut cream or heavy cream whipped with the almond extract and a teaspoon of powdered sugar if you like.

THERE IS NOTHING MORE DELIGHTFUL than this cold, refreshing bavarese to eat on a hot summer Sunday. In the summer, we like to eat at a table overlooking the sloping olive tree yard and the distant sea. When this cold cake is served, the smell of espresso spreads over the table. Its cool, soft, panna cotta–like top and cookie-like crust make the heat all the more enjoyable. You can make it vegan by using a vegan sponge cake and with coconut cream and almond milk instead of regular dairy.

COFFEE BAVARESE
A No-Bake "Cheesecake"

....

MAKES ONE 9-INCH (22 CM) PIE

....

One ¼-inch-thick (5 mm), 9-inch-diameter (22 cm) prepared sponge cake

2 tablespoons unsweetened cocoa powder

½ cup (125 ml) strong brewed coffee or espresso

3 egg yolks

2 cups (500 ml) whole milk or almond milk (preferably homemade)

2 cups (500 ml) heavy cream or coconut cream

2 tablespoons ground instant coffee

1 cup (7 oz/200 g) brown muscovado sugar

1 teaspoon vanilla extract

1 heaping tablespoon whole coffee beans, crushed (optional)

1 teaspoon (4 g) powdered agar-agar (see Note, page 220)

5 or 6 tablespoons (75 to 90 ml) warm water

Melted dark chocolate, for serving

1. Place the sponge cake in a 9-inch (22 cm) springform pan. Dissolve 1 tablespoon of the cocoa powder into the coffee and, using a brush, moisten the whole top of the sponge cake— you will likely not need all of the liquid. Dust the remaining 1 tablespoon cocoa powder over the sponge cake and set aside in the fridge.

2. Beat the egg yolks in a medium bowl with a stand or handheld mixer until pale and frothy, about 2 minutes. Place the milk, instant coffee, sugar, vanilla, and coffee beans (if using), in a small saucepan and heat over medium heat gently until the sugar is dissolved. Add the warm milk little by little to the egg yolks, stirring all the time. Pour the mixture back into the saucepan and heat, stirring almost continuously, until the mixture smokes—be careful not to boil it. Once smoking, turn off the heat, and whisk for a further minute.

3. In a separate small saucepan, dissolve the agar-agar in 1 tablespoon of the warm water. Add ½ cup (125 ml) of the warm water and bring to a boil over low heat, stirring constantly. Boil the agar-agar for 1 minute, until its slight seaweed smell subsides and it becomes a loose gel. If it starts to gel too quickly, remove from the heat and add another tablespoon of warm water.

recipe continues

NOTE: If you do not want to use agar-agar, you can omit it and make this cake a semifreddo, freezing it instead of refrigerating it. Just take it out of the freezer 10 to 15 minutes before slicing. It will have more of an ice cream–like texture.

4. While the milk-cream mixture is still hot, pour in the agar-agar gel. Stir to dissolve and combine well. (If there are specific instructions on how to use agar-agar powder on the package you purchased, make sure to follow those instead.)

5. Heat the mixture over medium heat for about 5 minutes, stirring slowly and constantly—do not boil. Let cool for about 10 minutes. (Be sure it's still warm—if it's too cool, the mixture will start curdling in the pan.) While it cools, beat the heavy cream with a stand or handheld mixer until stiff, and gently fold into the warm mixture.

6. Pour the mixture over the cake in the springform pan and transfer it back to the fridge. Let it set completely, for at least 4 hours or, even better, overnight. Serve cold with a drizzle of melted dark chocolate.

STREGA LIQUEUR, a sweet spirit made from more than seventy herbs including a hint of saffron, is a rather common and tasty addition to many sweet baked goods. But the idea of adding Strega to ricotta and making a delicious mousse came to an Italian pastry chef who christened it *ricotta stregata* (bewitched ricotta). You can use ricotta stregata to make a semifreddo (essentially an ice cream cake) by layering it with slices of sponge cake and chocolate chips and letting it set in the freezer. I cheat and make a single-serving version of it with hot roasted grapes on top, which really gives this dessert an Italian late-summer flair.

You can find Strega online or in an Italian specialty store. Use a tablespoon to flavor sponge cakes or any other cake (it goes well with any baked cake in this book) or as a substitute for rum.

"BEWITCHED" RICOTTA MOUSSE
With Roasted Balsamic Grapes

MAKES 8 SMALL GLASSES OR 6 LARGER GLASSES

For the roasted grapes:

1 pound (450 g) red grapes, preferably Concord or Red Globe seedless

1 tablespoon thick balsamic vinegar or glaze

3 tablespoons dark brown sugar, or 2 heaping tablespoons honey

1 tablespoon lemon juice

1 teaspoon vanilla extract

For the mousse:

1 heaping cup (10.5 oz/300 g) creamy ricotta

1 cup (250 ml) cold heavy cream

2 to 3 tablespoons honey or powdered brown sugar

2 tablespoons Strega liqueur

2 ounces (50 g) dark chocolate, finely chopped

2 amaretto cookies or your favorite cookie, plus more for decorating

Dark chocolate, to finish

1. **Make the roasted grapes:** Preheat the oven to 400°F (205°C). Cut the grapes in half and remove the seeds if there are any. In a medium bowl, whisk the vinegar, brown sugar, lemon juice, and vanilla together and add the grapes. Toss to coat well (for even better results, let them infuse overnight).

2. Add the grapes to a 11 × 7-inch (28 × 18-cm) baking dish and bake for about 20 minutes, until slightly caramelized. Toss the grapes halfway through the cooking time to avoid too much sticking. When they are finished cooking, there should still be some liquid in the pan.

3. **Make the mousse:** Mash the ricotta with a spatula with 1 tablespoon of the heavy cream until creamy. In a separate bowl, using a handheld or stand mixer, whip the rest of the cream with the honey and the Strega until firm. Fold one-third of the cream into the ricotta to make it fluffy. Gently fold in the rest of the heavy cream, along with the finely chopped chocolate.

recipe continues

TIP: What can you do if you can't find Strega? This recipe is delicious with Grand Marnier, St. Germain, Vin Santo, or any good rum. If you do not want to use any alcohol, use concord grape juice.

You can also substitute Savoiardi in lieu of the amaretti cookies. Break them to fit the size of your serving cup and soak them for a few seconds in the juices from the roasted grapes before layering. You can also use crumbled shortbread cookies.

4. Prepare 6 or 8 glasses or dessert cups: Crumble 1 amaretto cookie and divide it among the glasses or cups. Then divide half of the ricotta cream among the glasses or cups, crumble in the second cookie, and finish with the rest of the cream. Top with the roasted grapes and syrup, and some more crumbled cookies and shaved dark chocolate. Serve cold. You can even serve this with crumbled ice cream sugar cones.

FOR A FIG OR PEAR VARIATION: This recipe is also wonderful with figs or pears instead of grapes. Just use the same amount of sweet, ripe figs or sliced pears instead of the grapes.

TORTA DELLA NONNA is one of my all-time favorite and most requested recipes. I still remember the first time I ever made one: I was in New York and I wanted to make it for my host family. This recipe, which has been tried and tested many times over, is a staple in every kitchen throughout Italy—though its origins can be tracked in Liguria and Tuscany, where pine nuts abound. In this recipe, I give the classic cake a lemony twist, but should you want to make the traditional recipe, use less lemon or omit it entirely (see Variation).

TORTA DELLA NONNA
With Lemon Custard

MAKES ONE 9-INCH PIE

For the dough:

2¾ cups (12.3 oz/350 g) whole-wheat or spelt flour

¾ cup (3.5 oz/100 g) white wheat or spelt flour

¾ cup (3.5 oz/50 g) brown rice flour

Grated zest and juice of 1 medium lemon

1 teaspoon vanilla extract

2 cups (7 oz/200 g) packed light brown sugar

1 teaspoon baking soda

1 teaspoon baking powder

3 eggs

⅓ cup plus 1 tablespoon (100 ml) organic sunflower oil, plus more for greasing the pan

⅓ cup (75 ml) almond milk or regular milk, plus more to brush the top

For the assembly:

Lemon Custard (page 51), cooled

⅓ cup (1.4 oz/40 g) pine nuts

Candied lemon peel or candied ginger peel (optional)

1. Make the dough: Combine the flours, lemon zest and juice, vanilla, brown sugar, baking soda, baking powder, eggs, and sunflower oil in a food processor and process until the dough starts to come together (the dough will have large chunks). With the processor running, add a little bit of milk at a time to make the dough come together. (You might need more or less depending on what kind of flour you use.) If you are not using a food processor, just do the same in a bowl and knead by hand. The dough should be firm but quite sticky, almost difficult to work with without flour. Scrape it out of the bowl, wrap in plastic wrap, and refrigerate for at least 1 hour.

2. Preheat the oven to 350°F (180°C). Oil and flour a 9-inch (22 cm) pie pan.

3. Remove the dough from the fridge and divide it into two parts, one slightly smaller than the other. Roll each one out between two sheets of wax paper until it is about ¼ inch (5 mm) thick.

4. Line the pie pan with the larger dough disk, reversing it in with the help of the wax paper. Fill the pie with the custard, then cover with the other disk of dough and pinch the edges closed. Brush the top with milk and spread the pine nuts on top.

5. Bake for 35 to 40 minutes, or until golden on top. Wait for the cake to cool completely before slicing and serving. Even better make it the day before. Garnish with candied lemon peel or candied ginger strips.

FOR A CLASSIC TORTA DELLA NONNA: Use the grated zest of ½ lemon instead of 1 whole lemon in the dough, and use Classic Vanilla Custard (page 51) instead of the lemon custard.

THE ITALIAN PRESERVED PANTRY

How many jars of jams, vegetables in olive oil, and preserved fruit have come out of our kitchen! Every spring, summer, and fall, the women in our family (plus occasionally a friend) gather in the kitchen, armed with spoons and huge pots. With vats and baskets loaded with fresh produce, we get to work around a table so crowded with jars, peels, pits, and whatnot that we can barely see one another. I can hear the chatter, smell the strong vinegary scent of preserving vegetables, and the sweet smell of fruit and sugar. We always seem to get a few burned finger from being too eager to try the freshly cooked batches. Whatever we taste is always better than anything we can buy in a store.

Though it might seem intimidating at first, do try your hand at canning if you have access to good, organic produce. Canning your own fruit and vegetables is so rewarding, especially if you can do it with friends and family. It's worth it just for the memories you create.

PRESERVING & CANNING: GOOD PRACTICES

Choose organic, local, seasonal, good-quality produce. If you do not have your own fruit trees or garden but have access to a farmers' market, you will surely find an overload of great seasonal produce at a good price. All the recipes in this section make fairly small batches, but if you have never done any canning before, you can easily halve them and see how you like it.

Keep your workplace clean: Wash the fruit, dry it, have plenty of clean towels and all of your tools at the ready, wipe any spills, and be careful when boiling jars or jam, as they are extremely hot. Have all of your ingredients measured and ready. Start canning when you have plenty of time and are in no sort of rush.

Follow each step carefully and do not change the recipes: The amounts of acid, sugar, or salt are not only necessary for flavor and texture but for the actual preserving of the food. Unless you know what you're doing, do not alter the quantities.

TOOLS YOU WILL NEED:

- A large, tall pot, large enough to host all of the jars you will be using and to cover them with water

227

- Tea towels, one or two for boiling and one or two for drying
- Sturdy tongs for fishing out the jars
- Jars with perfectly fitting, unblemished lids

HOW TO STERILIZE JARS

Before you put any food into the jars, you will have to make sure they have been boiled and are dry.

Boiling the jars will kill bacteria, and you want to be sure there is no water left in the jars so no mold begins to form.

Boiling method

Start by placing the jars in the bottom of a tall pot that can fit them tight, and fit the lids in the empty spaces. Arrange a tea towel around the jars, draping it all around them so that they will be moving around as little as possible. Add water until the jars are completely covered by at least 3 inches (7.5 cm) and bring the water to a boil. Boil for 10 minutes.

Arrange one or two clean, dry tea towels on a work surface, turn off the heat, and fish out the jars with tongs, draining any excess water. Line the jars upside-down on the towels and wait until they are fully dry. To make sure they are completely dry, you can pop them in a preheated 325°F (160°C) oven for about 10 minutes.

Oven Method

Wash the jars with hot water and soap, rinse very well, and drain upside-down on kitchen towels. Preheat the oven to 325°F (160°C).

Line the jars (not the lids) on a rimmed baking sheet, making sure they do not touch, and pop them in the oven for 10 minutes.

Whichever method you decide to go for, once the jars are ready, sprinkle in some lemon juice and rub a piece of lemon around the rim.

Creating an acidic environment will increase the safety of your canned goods.

A BASIC GUIDE TO CANNING

Upside-down method for jams & sauces

This method is the easiest and works well for jams or any liquid that has been boiling for more than 10 minutes. It works well with lidded jars. Have your sterilized jars and kitchen towels ready. Pour the hot mixture into the jars, leaving a 1-inch (2.5-cm) space at the top. Twist the lids closed and turn the jars upside down. Let them cool completely, then flip them back over. Test the lids by pressing a finger in the center: They should be firm and not produce a popping sound. If they do pop, or if you can screw off the lids too easily, proceed to the boiling method described below.

The sealed jars last several months in the pantry. Consume within a year.

Boiling method

This method works exactly like sterilizing the jars: Put the jars in the bottom of a pot that can fit them tightly, arrange a tea towel around them to reduce impact, and cover with water by at least 3 inches (7.5 cm). Bring to a rolling boil, and boil for 10 minutes. Turn off the heat and leave the jars in the pot for 5 additional minutes.

Fish out the jars with tongs and place them upright on a double layer of tea towels. Let them cool completely.

How do I know my cans have been sealed properly?

When the jars cool, press your finger on the lid. It should not produce any clicking sound when pressed or flex in or out. If it doesn't, your jars have been sealed properly and the vacuum has been created. If it does click, you should repeat the boiling process.

When you open the jars, the lid should produce a noisy "click" and you should clearly hear the sound of air being sucked in. Opening well-sealed jars is quite difficult, so if the jars open too easily, they might have been poorly sealed.

If, after sitting in your pantry for a while, the lids inflate or move, you might not have canned your goods properly. If they smell weird, change color, or seem altered in any way, do not consume.

Canning will prevent the development of molds and bacteria, but it will not stop the growth of a pathogen called botulinum, which might develop if the heat is too low or the acidity level of the food is too low. Because all of the recipes in this section contain acidic agents such as lemon, vinegar, and sugar, there is no need to worry about botulinum if the sealing is done properly.

Also, luckily, botulinum will not go unnoticed: Its growth will cause your canned goods to produce gas and smell rotten.

However, please keep in mind that, even though people have been canning for centuries, there's no 100 percent safety guarantee when it comes to home canning. Always be very careful in each step of each recipe.

———————————————————————

Balsamic Onions for Cooking & Preserving (V/GF) • Marinated Olives (V/GF)

Zucchini in Olive Oil (V/GF) • Tomato Passata (V/GF)

Preserved Apricots & Other Fruits in Vanilla & Rum Syrup (V/GF)

Stone Fruit Jam: Peach, Plum, Apricot, Cherry (V/GF)

Drying Your Own Herbs • Infusing Extra-Virgin Olive Oil

IN MY OPINION (and not only mine), balsamic onions are one of the most versatile, delicious basics of Italian cooking. Used equally by food trucks, fancy restaurants, and home cooks, you could add them to potentially any recipe in this book save for the desserts. I love to make them and use them as is, but with more sugar they can easily be converted to a delicious compote you can enjoy with cheeses or antipasti platters or on bruschetta. Below are the instructions for both versions.

BALSAMIC ONIONS
For Cooking & Preserving

....
MAKES ONE 10-FLUID-OUNCE (300-MILLILITER) JAR
....

1 pound (450 g) red onions (Tropea variety, if you can find them)

1 tablespoon olive oil

½ scant cup (100 ml) balsamic vinegar

1 heaping tablespoon honey

3 tablespoons (2.5 oz/30 g) packed dark brown sugar

1 scant teaspoon salt

Additional spices: 3 or 4 juniper berries, a pinch of ground cinnamon, a pinch of ground ginger (optional)

If making Balsamic Onion Compote for preserving:

¾ cup (5.3 oz/150 g) packed dark brown sugar

1. Cut off both ends of the onions and peel the onions. Slice them in half, then into very fine half-moons—you can use a mandoline slicer to make it easier and even.

2. Place the olive oil in a large pan and add the onions. Sauté over medium heat for about 5 minutes, until the onions soften. Add the vinegar, stir well, and let the onions soften for 10 minutes, stirring halfway through. Once the onions are soft, add the honey, brown sugar, salt, and spices if using and stir well to dissolve the sweeteners. If you are planning to make a compote and jar these onions, add the extra ¾ cup (5.3 oz/150 g) brown sugar.

3. Reduce the heat to very low, cover the pan, and cook for 45 minutes, stirring every now and then. The onions should have a rich and creamy consistency rather than caramelize.

4. Once thickened and creamy, the onions are ready to use for cooking or ready to be jarred (see instructions on page 228).

NOTE: If using for cooking: Use them to make the Chickpea "Frittata" with Red Onions (page 64), as a topping for Bruschetta (page 45) or Quick Pizza (page 46) or Polenta al Tagliere Three Ways: Beans, Mushroom Sauce, Truffle Oil (page 112), on the Emilia-Style Vegetable Burgers (page 205), just eat with cheese, or with anything that strikes your fancy!

THESE OLIVES ARE A GREAT ADDITION TO SALADS, antipasti platters, veggie burgers, croquettes, and even pasta. I've also included a variation with cheese, which is delicious smothered on top of Bruschetta (page 45).

MARINATED OLIVES

MAKES TWO 1-CUP (250-ML) JARS

¼ cup (a full cupped hand) packed fresh parsley or basil, or both, finely minced

1 teaspoon whole peppercorns

Olive oil, enough to cover (1 to 1½ cup/250 to 375 mo)

1 heaping cup (250 to 300 ml) of your favorite pitted black, green, or mixed olives

2 garlic cloves, finely minced

1 tablespoon capers, rinsed and chopped

1 teaspoon dried oregano

Grated zest of ½ small lemon

3 or 4 fresh basil leaves

1. Add one-third of the parsley and half the peppercorns to the bottom of a canning jar. Pour in about ¼ cup (50 ml) olive oil and add half the olives. Sprinkle on half the garlic, another third of the parsley, and the remaining peppercorns, half the capers, half the oregano, the lemon zest, and 2 torn basil leaves. Cover with olive oil, and repeat, using up all of the ingredients. Store in the fridge.

2. After a day, the olive oil should have reduced. Cover the olives in oil again. As long as they are submerged in oil, they will keep in the fridge for 2 to 3 weeks.

3. If you want to jar them to store in your pantry, follow the directions for sterilizing the jars on page 228.

TO MAKE MARINATED CHEESE AND OLIVES: Double the recipe and add 1 cup (4.5 oz/130 g) cubed hard cheese, such as feta or goat's cheese. Marinate for 1 day before consuming, and keep covered in oil. Customize the marinade with your favorite herbs.

HAVING A VEGETABLE GARDEN means that we have more zucchini in the summer than one family can possibly manage, so this recipe has been a staple in my household for years. And when I say years, I mean that it was passed down to us from my great-grandmother, so it has been tested quite well by now. If you don't have a garden, this is the perfect recipe for a load of zucchini you can find cheaply at your local farmer's market in the summer. These zucchini are wonderful as a pizza topping, sandwich stuffing instead of pickles, and even in salads. The recipe takes several days to prepare—I like to start in the morning so that it's easy to complete the next steps over the following few mornings.

ZUCCHINI IN OLIVE OIL

MAKES THREE OR FOUR 10-FLUID-OUNCE (300-ML) JARS

6½ pounds (about 3 kg) zucchini

Plenty of salt

2 cups (500 ml) white wine vinegar

2 cups (500 ml) water

2 cups (500 ml) white wine

3 or 4 garlic cloves, finely chopped (1 per jar)

¾ to 1 cup (1.5 to 2.1 oz/45 to 60 g) fresh basil or parsley, finely chopped (¼ cup/15 g per jar)

3 or 4 teaspoons dried oregano (1 teaspoon per jar)

3 or 4 pieces dried red pepper flakes (1 piece per jar)

3 or 4 teaspoons peppercorns (1 teaspoon per jar)

Plenty of olive oil (4 to 6 cups/ about 1l; see Note, page 236)

Day 1, Morning

1. Start by preparing the zucchini: Cut the ends off, cut them in half lengthwise, then in half again lengthwise. Cut off the core by slicing the white part lengthwise, and cut each slice into half-moons that are slightly thicker than ⅛ inch (3 mm).

2. Prepare a colander (or two if your colander is small). Add one layer of zucchini on the bottom and sprinkle with 2 pinches of salt. Add another layer and repeat. Continue until all of the zucchini have been added to the colander. Let the zucchini drain for 24 hours.

Day 2, Morning

1. Prepare a clean cotton kitchen towel.

2. Place the vinegar, water, and wine to a large pot and bring to a boil over medium heat. Squeeze the zucchini with your hands over the sink to remove any excess water and add to the pot. Boil for 5 minutes, until softened. Drain, and slightly press the zucchini with the back of a spoon to get rid of some excess liquid.

3. Spread the kitchen towel on a work surface and add the zucchini. Roll the kitchen towel into a log, so that you can grab

recipe continues

NOTE: You do not need high-quality olive oil for canning vegetables, but even with half-decent olive oil the process can be a little expensive. You can use half vegetable oil and half good olive oil instead, and it will still taste great. If you can, I encourage you to choose organic oils.

both ends. Twist to squeeze out as much liquid as possible. Place the zucchini in the towel in the colander for 6 hours, then transfer to a clean kitchen towel and repeat, changing to a clean towel each time. Before bed, change the towel again and repeat, then let the zucchini drip overnight.

Day 3, Morning

1. Sterilize the jars as per instruction on page 228.

2. When the jars are cool enough to handle, prepare the garlic, basil, red pepper flakes, peppercorns, and olive oil, so that you have them ready.

3. Add a 1-inch (2.5-cm) layer of zucchini to the bottom of each jar, then sprinkle half of the garlic, half of the herbs, half of the peppercorns, and a small pinch red pepper flakes, or more or less depending on how much spice you like. Add another 1-inch (2.5-cm) layer of zucchini and repeat with the rest of the garlic, herbs, and peppercorns. Add another layer of zucchini, enough to leave a 1½-inch (4-cm) space at the top. Add enough olive oil to completely cover the zucchini by at least ½ inch (1.5 cm). Make sure nothing sticks out of the oil. Repeat with the other jars.

4. When you are done, close the jars well and store them in a dark place. Check them after one day: If the oil has reduced, add more—the zucchini should always be fully covered with oil. Check them again after a couple of days, adding more oil to keep them covered.

5. The zucchini can be safely stored in a dark cupboard or pantry for 3 months. Once opened, store them in the fridge and make sure the zucchini is always covered in oil. If you want to be 100 percent safe, or want to store them for longer, boil the jars according to the instructions on page 228. This way, they will keep for up to a year.

FOR AN EGGPLANT VARIATION: You can make this recipe using eggplants by following the same procedure. Choose long, small eggplants rather than the round kind.

WHAT WOULD AN ITALIAN PERSON DO without tomato-based sauces—even when it's winter and fresh tomatoes are but a far memory? My family has been making tomato passata for as long as I can remember, and it really is our most used year-round staple.

If you have access to ripe, juicy tomatoes, it is worth making your own tomato passata—especially if you cannot find it anywhere near you. Making it is easy and, if sealed, it can be stored for up to a year in a dark place. The recipe can be easily multiplied.

TOMATO PASSATA

MAKES ABOUT 6 CUPS (1.5 L)

4½ pounds (2 kg) ripe, red, juicy tomatoes (preferably of the San Marzano variety)

Fresh basil leaves, 2 for each jar you are using

1. Wash the tomatoes and dry them with a kitchen towel.

2. Cut the tomatoes in half and remove the seeds, then transfer to a large pot and cover. Cook over low heat for about 10 minutes, until the tomatoes soften and release their water.

3. Either pass the tomatoes through a food mill or process in a blender (preferably a high-speed blender, so you will be sure there will be no bits of skins). Return the tomatoes to the pot and bring to a boil over medium heat. Cook for 10 minutes more, until thickened.

4. Have your sterilized jars ready according to instructions on page 228. Add 2 torn basil leaves per jar and pour in the hot tomato passata, leaving 1 inch (2.5 cm) at the top. It is best to use the boiling method for tomato passata rather than the inversion method, as the tomato might not get hot enough to produce a proper seal.

THIS IS AN ESSENTIAL RECIPE when our trees are way too loaded with fruit from early summer to fall, and it works well with pretty much any kind of fruit (though I find that preserving stone fruit gives the best results). Vanilla is lovely, but experiment with adding your favorite spices to taste.

PRESERVED APRICOTS & OTHER FRUITS
In Vanilla & Rum Syrup

MAKES SIX 17-FLUID-OUNCE (500-ML) JARS

4½ pounds (2 kg) fresh apricots (see Note if using other fruit)

2 cups (14 oz/400 g) packed dark brown sugar

⅓ cup (75 ml) plus 1 tablespoon (15 ml) lemon juice

8 cups (2 l) water

2 vanilla beans, seeds scraped

2 to 3 tablespoons rum per jar

Extra spices: cinnamon stick, star anise, crushed cardamom cloves

1. Have your sterilized jars ready, according to the instructions on page 228.

2. Thoroughly wash the apricots, dry them thoroughly, cut them in half, and remove and discard the pits.

3. Put the apricots in a large bowl with half the brown sugar and 1 tablespoon of the lemon juice. Toss to coat well.

4. Place the water, remaining sugar, remaining ⅓ cup (75 ml) lemon juice, and the vanilla bean pods and seeds in a large pot. Bring to a boil over medium heat.

5. Once boiling, reduce to a simmer and add the apricots, scraping into the pot all of the juices and sugar in the bottom of the bowl. Blanch the apricots for 30 seconds, then immediately drain with a slotted spoon or sieve and return them to the bowl.

6. Continue cooking the syrup over medium-high heat for about 30 minutes, until reduced by half.

7. When you are ready to jar the fruit, divide the apricots evenly into the jars. Push down with a spoon so that there is as little empty space and air as possible, and leave 1 inch (2.5 cm) at the top of each jar. Divide the syrup among the jars, making

sure the fruit is well covered. In each jar, add the rum, a piece of the vanilla pod you used for cooking, and, if you like, a ½-inch (1.5 cm) piece of cinnamon and 1 star anise. Seal, and sterilize the jars according to the instructions on page 228.

FOR PRESERVED PEARS AND APPLES: Follow the instructions above, but peel pears and/or apples before blanching. Add a whole stick of cinnamon per jar for added flavor.

FOR PRESERVED PEACHES: Blanch peaches for 1 minute, then peel off the skin.

FOR PRESERVED CHERRIES: There is no need for blanching. Just wash, dry, and pit cherries, and add to the jars, then cover them with the hot syrup.

FOR PRESERVED BERRIES: Do not blanch. Add berries to the jar whole before covering in hot syrup.

THE SMELL OF JAM COOKING in my grandma's large, tall pots is a strong memory from all my childhood years, and now that I am an adult I still love to lick the spoon right after the jam is done, smother some right on a slice of homemade bread, and enjoy the blissful mix of deliciousness and nostalgia. This recipe works well with any stone fruit—perfect if you have a fruit tree that will inundate your kitchen with more produce than you can consume in a few days.

STONE FRUIT JAM
Peach, Plum, Apricot, Cherry

MAKES 4 TO 5 CUPS (1L TO 1.25 L)

4½ pounds (2 kg) organic peaches (or any other stone fruit), some a bit on the unripe side

1 small green apple, cored and cubed

Juice of 1 medium lemon

8 cups (1.7 pounds/800 g) packed dark brown sugar

1 cup (250 ml) pure, unfiltered apple juice

¼ cup (50 ml) rum, 1 whole vanilla bean (optional)

1. Sterilize the jars according to the instructions on page 228.

2. Wash the peaches and apple thoroughly, and rub the peaches well to rid them of the fuzz on the skin (not necessary if using nectarines or other stone fruit). Cut the peaches and apple into pieces and add to a large pot that can fit them and leave some space on top. Toss with the lemon juice, a third of the sugar, the apple juice, and the rum and vanilla bean if using. Soak the fruit in its own juice for 24 hours, covering the pot with a tea towel.

3. When ready, place the pot over medium heat. Let the fruit juice come to a boil, reduce to heat to medium-low, and cook for 15 minutes, stirring every now and then.

4. Using an immersion blender, or transferring the fruit to a regular blender, blend the fruit until smooth. Return the fruit to the pot, add another third of the sugar, and cook over medium-low heat for about 20 minutes. Skim the foam that will rise to the surface if you want a completely clear-looking jam.

5. Add the remaining third of the sugar and raise the heat to medium. At this point, you should not leave the pot. Stir regularly every 2 minutes to avoid sticking. Within 5 to 10 minutes, the jam should thicken and easily coat a spoon.

6. To test the jam for doneness, add a tablespoonful to a small dish and tilt it: If the jam runs down too quickly, it needs to cook longer. If it does not budge, it means the sugar has caramelized too much and it is overcooked. If these happens, you can try to loosen it up by stirring in a cup of hot water. Ideally, the jam should run down slowly and with some resistance: That is when you know it is perfectly done. Keep in mind that the jam will thicken further as it cools.

7. Fill the jars, leaving 1 inch (2.5 cm) from the brim, and seal. You can jar them using the upside-down method (see page 228). If you want to eat some right away, store in the fridge once cool and consume within a week.

JAM-MAKING TIPS

• This recipe will work well with any kind of stone fruit. Depending on how sour the fruit is, you can add more or less sugar: If using plums or prunes, add ½ to 1 cup (3.5 to 7 oz./ 100 to 200 g) more sugar.

• Choose organic fruit and keep the skin on, washing it very thoroughly. The skin contains pectin, which is what makes your jam thicken. To increase the amount of pectin, choose 3 or 4 pieces of fruit that are not completely ripe.

• If you want to double or triple the recipe, cook in separate batches. Cooking more than 5 pounds (2 kg) of fruit in one go will take a very long time.

• If your jam looks like it is not thickening, just cook it longer or add another ½ cup (100 g) of sugar.

DRYING YOUR OWN HERBS

Having dried herbs in the pantry year-round can save you some grocery store trips. It is an easy thing to do, provided you have a dry place away from direct sunlight to keep them in. If you don't, you can dry your herbs in the oven.

Pick the herbs before they flower and in the morning to get the maximum concentration of flavor and essential oils. Then pick them again before the end of the season, so you have them trimmed for the winter. Pick them by cutting the stalks close to the base, and making small bunches that are similar in size.

Before you begin, wash and dry your herbs thoroughly by gently patting them with clean kitchen towels.

TRADITIONAL METHOD

After picking, washing, and drying the herbs thoroughly, group in bunches and tie at the base with kitchen twine. Hang them upside down in an aerated, dry place, away from direct sunlight. Turn the bunches on their sides once a day to dry them as evenly as possible. The herbs are ready when they break and crumble to the touch.

Depending on the kind of herb, it might take anywhere from 5 days to over 2 weeks. Fresh herbs such as basil and parsley will take the longest, while woodsy herbs such as rosemary and thyme will dry more quickly and will probably be ready in just 1 to 2 weeks, depending on how dry the room and weather are.

OVEN METHOD

Line a rimmed baking sheet with parchment paper. After washing and drying your herbs, separate each stem or branch and line them on the baking sheet without overlapping too much. Dry on the lowest setting your oven can go—not above 175°F (80°C)—and dry, turning the herbs every 30 minutes, then every 15 minutes, until crumbly and crisp. Depending on the kind of herb, it might take anywhere from 45 minutes to well over 1 hour.

With this method, you can only dry one kind of herb at a time, as each herb will take a different amount of time to dry.

Once your herbs are dried, you can either store them whole in glass jars or grind them in a mortar and pestle. Whole herbs will maintain their properties for longer, but ground herbs can be a little easier to store. Store all dried herbs away from sunlight and humidity.

INFUSING EXTRA-VIRGIN OLIVE OIL

Infused olive oil makes not only a wonderful addition to simple dressings or a perfect finish for salads, soups, and vegetables, but it also makes a wonderful gift when presented in small, pretty bottles. A friend from Tuscany always tells me how she loves to lunch on sourdough bread and extra-virgin olive oil alone when November comes and the new olive oil is pressed. Infused olive oil makes you want to do just that. Also, there is nothing that will up your bruschetta game as much as a good oil. There are two ways to make infused oils.

1ST METHOD: COLD INFUSION

You will need:

- Perfectly clean and dry glass jars
- Spices as desired (see Variations, page 247)
- 1 cup (250 ml) extra-virgin olive oil

Add the herbs or spices to the jar, pour the olive oil over them, and make sure the flavorings are completely submerged, or they might develop mold. Close the jars tightly and leave in a cool, dark place for at least 1 week and up to 1 month, depending on the flavoring you are using. Shake the jar every couple of days or so. Make sure the herbs and spices remain constantly submerged in the oil, pushing them to the bottom of the jars.

Taste the oil and, when you are happy with the flavor, filter it through a sieve with a paper napkin, and then into a clean bottle using a funnel. Let it take its time—it might take hours to drip completely into the bottle. When done, squeeze out the oil left in the herbs or flavorings, then discard the herbs.

Let the jar stand for a whole 24 hours, so that all of the residue falls to the bottom. At this point you can filter it again or leave as is. If you do not have a dark bottle or jar, wrap the bottle in aluminum foil to keep the light from reaching the oil.

2ND METHOD: WARM INFUSION

Infusing the olive oil in warm water will get the job done in about 2 hours but, because extra-virgin olive oil is extremely sensitive to temperature changes, some of its nutritional values will inevitably be lost—especially its many healthy antioxidants. Still, it is a nice quick fix if time is your main concern.

If you are using dried herbs, add them to a jar with the oil and close the jar with its lid. If you are using fresh herbs, do not lid the jar, so

recipe continues

the water from the herbs can evaporate. Add the jars to a pot, keeping them upright, and add enough hot water to cover the jars by half. Put the pot over the lowest heat setting possible and let it infuse for 4 hours. The heat should be so low that you shouldn't see much steam coming off the water. Turn off the heat every 30 minutes or so, let the temperature go down for about 10 minutes, and turn on the heat again, to avoid overheating.

When ready, take the jars out of the water and let them cool completely before filtering the oils into dark bottles and in a dark place.

Infused olive oil will last about 3 months. When the oil starts to lose its aroma or smell rancid, it means it has been sitting for too long. Always properly store the oils away from heat and direct sunlight.

INFUSED OLIVE OIL VARIATIONS:

BASIL OLIVE OIL: Add the basil to a jar and pour the olive oil over the basil. Infuse for 20 days in a dark place, or infuse with the warm infusion method.

GARLIC OLIVE OIL: Garlic oil takes the shortest time. Peel and crush 4 or 5 large garlic cloves per cup (250 ml) of oil and infuse overnight. If left for too long, the garlic flavor becomes overpowering and it tastes rancid. Fish out the garlic as soon as you think the oil is ready. It is great on bruschetta or in any preparation where raw garlic is too powerful for your taste.

CHILI OIL: Add 2 to 4 crushed Italian dried chilies to a cup (250 ml) of oil, depending on how strong you like it, and infuse for 2 days before using. There is no need to filter chili oil—just leave the chili pieces floating in the bottom of the bottle.

ROSEMARY OLIVE OIL: Add ¼ cup (0.35 oz/ 10 g) dried rosemary to 1 cup (250 ml) olive oil,

or use 1 or 2 fresh rosemary sprigs. Infuse for at least 3 weeks before using. Great on chickpeas and in hearty fall and winter soups.

LEMON OLIVE OIL: Cut the skin from 1 small organic lemon, trying to get as little of the white part as possible, and add to 1 cup (250 ml) olive oil. Infuse in a dark place for 10 to 12 days, and filter into a clean bottle. Add some clementine zest to the infusion for a more interesting citrus flavor.

OLIVE OIL FOR PASTA: Add 2 crushed dried Italian chilies, 2 peeled and crushed garlic cloves, and a ¼ cup (0.35 oz/10 g) mix of dried basil, parsley, and a pinch of oregano. These flavors are very commonly used to dress a simple bowl of pasta.

MIXED HERBS OLIVE OIL: Add ¼ cup (0.35 oz/10 g) mixed dried herbs such as basil, parsley, oregano, marjoram, and thyme to 1 cup (250 ml) olive oil. Infuse for 3 weeks before filtering.

ACKNOWLEDGMENTS

This book is dedicated to my mother, the most kind, inspiring, hard-working (and probably short-tempered) woman I know. None of my work would have happened without your support, and without all the times you kept cooking for and with me even though you really wanted to sit down and rest. Thank you for supporting me and helping me make sense of all the teaspoons and tablespoons.

To my grandparents, my dad, and all of my family: Thanks for being the best storytellers, and for constantly pushing me on the swing of life. This book happened thanks to your knowledge as well.

To Jon: None of what I have done would have happened without you. You taught me to believe that I can achieve everything I want and, even if I have ways to go in life, you taught me how to find, and stick to, my True North. If I resemble anything close to a woman, it is thanks to you. To you and your family, I will be forever grateful.

To all my blogger friends: I often stop and think what my life would be today without you all and I couldn't even imagine it. Over time, so many fellow bloggers have reached out to me and now it feels like family. To Zaira and Francesco specifically, who gracefully let me enter their lives; and to Betty, Christiann, Anisa, and the many others I met along the way. Every single one of you whom I've met in person and had a chance to talk to, I thank you endlessly for your very existence. Thank you for making me feel at home wherever I go.

To all my readers: thank you for trusting me and following my work. You have seen me evolve into a professional and I feel elated and humbled that so many of you are still around to watch me share photos of vegetables and flowers. Maybe one day you'll get sick of it. But for now, thank you for everything. This book would never have happened without you.

And to the team behind this book: Berta, Lucia, Nina, and Ashley: Thank you for believing in me in spite of my insecurities, which led to delays and many reshoots. This book is beautiful thanks to your work. See you one day in the Italian countryside!